D0123527

sexual violence

OPPOSING VIEWPOINTS®

David L. Bender, *Publisher*

Bruno Leone, *Executive Editor*

Scott Barbour, *Managing Editor*

Brenda Stalcup, *Senior Editor*

Mary E. Williams, *Book Editor*

Tamara L. Roleff, *Book Editor*

OPPOSING
VIEWPOINTS®
SERIES

Greenhaven Press, Inc., San Diego, California

Cover photo: Craig MacLain

Library of Congress Cataloging-in-Publication Data

Sexual violence : opposing viewpoints / Mary E. Williams, Tamara L.
    Roleff, editors.
        p.   cm. — (Opposing viewpoints series)
    Includes bibliographical references and index.
    ISBN 1-56510-560-5 — ISBN 1-56510-559-1 (pbk. : alk. paper)
    1. Sex crimes. 2. Women—Crimes against. 3. Sexual abuse victims.
4. Violent crimes—Prevention. I. Williams, Mary E., 1960–   . II. Roleff, Tamara L., 1959–   . III. Series: Opposing viewpoints series (Un-
numbered)
HQ71.S414 1997
364.15'3—dc21   96-40122
                                                                    CIP

Greenhaven Press, Inc., P.O. Box 289009
San Diego, CA 92198-9009

"CONGRESS SHALL MAKE NO LAW... ABRIDGING THE FREEDOM OF SPEECH, OR OF THE PRESS."

First Amendment to the U.S. Constitution

The basic foundation of our democracy is the First Amendment guarantee of freedom of expression. The Opposing Viewpoints Series is dedicated to the concept of this basic freedom and the idea that it is more important to practice it than to enshrine it.

CONTENTS

Chapter 3: How Should Society Address Sexual Victimization?

Chapter 4: How Can Sexual Violence Be Reduced?

WHY CONSIDER OPPOSING VIEWPOINTS?

"The only way in which a human being can make some approach to knowing the whole of a subject is by hearing what can be said about it by persons of every variety of opinion and studying all modes in which it can be looked at by every character of mind. No wise man ever acquired his wisdom in any mode but this."

John Stuart Mill

In our media-intensive culture it is not difficult to find differing opinions. Thousands of newspapers and magazines and dozens of radio and television talk shows resound with differing points of view. The difficulty lies in deciding which opinion to agree with and which "experts" seem the most credible. The more inundated we become with differing opinions and claims, the more essential it is to hone critical reading and thinking skills to evaluate these ideas. Opposing Viewpoints books address this problem directly by presenting stimulating debates that can be used to enhance and teach these skills. The varied opinions contained in each book examine many different aspects of a single issue. While examining these conveniently edited opposing views, readers can develop critical thinking skills such as the ability to compare and contrast authors' credibility, facts, argumentation styles, use of persuasive techniques, and other stylistic tools. In short, the Opposing Viewpoints Series is an ideal way to attain the higher-level thinking and reading skills so essential in a culture of diverse and contradictory opinions.

In addition to providing a tool for critical thinking, Opposing Viewpoints books challenge readers to question their own strongly held opinions and assumptions. Most people form their opinions on the basis of upbringing, peer pressure, and personal, cultural, or professional bias. By reading carefully balanced opposing views, readers must directly confront new ideas as well as the opinions of those with whom they disagree. This is not to simplistically argue that everyone who reads opposing views will—or should—change his or her opinion. Instead, the series enhances readers' understanding of their own views by encouraging confrontation with opposing ideas. Careful examination of others' views can lead to the readers' understanding of the logical inconsistencies in their own opinions, perspective on why they hold an opinion, and the consideration of the possibility that their opinion requires further evaluation.

EVALUATING OTHER OPINIONS

To ensure that this type of examination occurs, Opposing Viewpoints books present all types of opinions. Prominent spokespeople on different sides of each issue as well as well-known professionals from many disciplines challenge the reader. An additional goal of the series is to provide a forum for other, less known, or even unpopular viewpoints. The opinion of an ordinary person who has had to make the decision to cut off life support from a terminally ill relative, for example, may be just as valuable and provide just as much insight as a medical ethicist's professional opinion. The editors have two additional purposes in including these less known views. One, the editors encourage readers to respect others' opinions—even when not enhanced by professional credibility. It is only by reading or listening to and objectively evaluating others' ideas that one can determine whether they are worthy of consideration. Two, the inclusion of such viewpoints encourages the important critical thinking skill of objectively evaluating an author's credentials and bias. This evaluation will illuminate an author's reasons for taking a particular stance on an issue and will aid in readers' evaluation of the author's ideas.

As series editors of the Opposing Viewpoints Series, it is our hope that these books will give readers a deeper understanding of the issues debated and an appreciation of the complexity of even seemingly simple issues when good and honest people disagree. This awareness is particularly important in a democratic society such as ours in which people enter into public debate to determine the common good. Those with whom one disagrees should not be regarded as enemies but rather as people whose views deserve careful examination and may shed light on one's own.

Thomas Jefferson once said that "difference of opinion leads to inquiry, and inquiry to truth." Jefferson, a broadly educated man, argued that "if a nation expects to be ignorant and free . . . it expects what never was and never will be." As individuals and as a nation, it is imperative that we consider the opinions of others and examine them with skill and discernment. The Opposing Viewpoints Series is intended to help readers achieve this goal.

David L. Bender & Bruno Leone,
Series Editors

INTRODUCTION

"Few other human transgressions elicit the level of anger, fear and distaste that many Americans feel in response to sexual crimes."

—Erica Goode

In the last three decades of the twentieth century, rape, sexual assault, sexual abuse, and child molestation have increasingly become the focus of public concern. According to a 1993 National Crime Victimization Survey conducted by the U.S. Department of Justice, about 500,000 rapes or sexual assaults occur each year. Child protective services report approximately 200,000 substantiated cases of child sexual abuse annually. Moreover, the Department of Justice states that since 1985, "rape rates have risen nearly three times as fast as the total crime rate." Although various other studies offer statistics that conflict with these numbers—for example, the National Women's Study claims that about 683,000 rapes of adult women occur annually, while the Federal Bureau of Investigation reports 103,000 such rapes each year—most lawmakers and experts agree that sexual violence is a problem requiring persistent attention and investigation.

In the 1990s, a number of violent crimes committed by released sex offenders received wide media attention and prompted many states to pass laws specifying that communities must be notified about paroled sex criminals living in the area. In addition, some states decided to detain particularly violent sex offenders for mental treatment after they have served out their prison sentences. These measures reflect the public's fear that released sex criminals will commit further offenses. According to CQ Researcher writer Sarah Glazer, even though "experts assert that recidivism rates vary among different kinds of sex offenders" and only "a minority of sex offenders offend again," much of the public, as well as many lawmakers, remains unconvinced that releasing sex criminals is a sound policy. Increasingly, many debates on the issue of sexual violence focus on whether or not sex offenders can be effectively rehabilitated.

One approach to rehabilitation that is gaining popularity in various states is "chemical castration"—the use of Depo-Provera, a drug that decreases the level of the hormone testosterone in men. Lowered testosterone levels lead to a dramatic decrease in sexual thoughts and fantasies, proponents of Depo-Provera argue, and can often eliminate a sex offender's urge to commit sexual crimes. For example, Steven, a Maryland rapist who received Depo-Provera injections during and after his incarceration, maintains that his treatment has been successful: "The will to have sex [is] still there. . . . But Depo-Provera allows you the time, mentally, to make the decision about whether this is an appropriate behavior. . . . Sex doesn't control me anymore."

Other supporters of Depo-Provera point out that in countries requiring surgical or chemical castration for sex offenders, the recidivism rate of child molesters has dropped from nearly 100 percent to 2 percent. Moreover, they argue, tests conducted in the United States report a repeat-offense rate of only 5 percent for sex criminals treated with the drug. In the opinion of Douglas J. Besharov of the American Enterprise Institute, "The use of hormone-suppressing drugs . . . holds great promise for reducing the level of sexual violence against women and children." Besharov contends that the use of Depo-Provera provides assurance that the sex criminal will not be a threat to the community that becomes his home after his release.

Many medical experts and psychologists caution, however, that the usefulness of Depo-Provera is limited. Fred Berlin, director of the National Institute for the Study, Prevention, and Treatment of Sexual Trauma, maintains that the drug works only for a subgroup of sex offenders—those whose crimes are driven by overwhelming sexual urges rather than by violent tendencies or by psychosis. Furthermore, he argues, "all studies on the drug's effectiveness have been in carefully controlled settings, with men motivated to use it, and in conjunction with counseling and other follow-up therapy." In other words, experts warn, the use of Depo-Provera alone does not guarantee a low rate of repeat offenses.

Opponents of the use of Depo-Provera note that the drug has many potentially damaging side effects, including weight gain, hypertension, and diabetes. These critics argue that it is unfair to use a treatment that may involve life-threatening health complications, particularly since released sex offenders have already been punished for their crimes by serving prison sentences. Moreover, these commentators contend, some sex criminals must stop the weekly injections because of the severe side effects. Since stopping the drug treatment causes hormonal levels to return to their former heights, thereby increasing the risk for repeat offenses, sex criminals in these cases must be monitored closely. These offenders end up having to choose one of three options: continue to suffer side effects, return to jail, or agree to surgical castration. The third option is deemed "cruel and unusual punishment" by the American Civil Liberties Union (ACLU). Carole Migden, a California assemblywoman, agrees with the ACLU in its opposition to both chemical and surgical castration: "There has to be another way. In the name of humanity, it is wrong for the government to mutilate the bodies of our citizens."

Other critics also question the rationale for using either chemical or surgical castration to treat sex offenders. According to Denise Snyder, executive director of the Washington, D.C., Rape Crisis Center, supporters of castration "misfocus the issue and feed into the myths about rape. Sexual assault is a crime of violence and aggression . . . not the product of an uncontrollable sex drive." Furthermore, argues Barbara Schwartz, director of the Sex Offender Treatment program at Two Rivers Correctional Center in Monroe, Washington, a castrated rapist "could still be a phenomenal danger. He can go out and . . . [sexually] assault [people] with broom handles or bottles or beat them up or kill them." Sheila Kuehl of the California State Assembly agrees: "A person who has been castrated is still able to molest a child. [Molesters] need to be kept out of society—kept away."

Despite these objections to the use of Depo-Provera, chemical castration as a treatment for sex offenders is gaining widespread support. In January 1997, California became the first state to require the chemical castration of twice-convicted child molesters, and several other states are considering similar measures. As such measures are implemented, the controversy over chemical castration is likely to increase. The authors in Sexual Violence: Opposing Viewpoints present differing opinions on this issue of offender rehabilitation as well as debate about the causes, effects, and prevalence of sexual violence in the following chapters: What Causes Sexual Violence? How Serious a Problem Is Sexual Violence? How Should Society Address Sexual Victimization? How Can Sexual Violence Be Reduced?

CHAPTER 1

WHAT CAUSES SEXUAL VIOLENCE?

CHAPTER PREFACE

Most sports require athletes to be aggressive on the field. Some athletes carry their aggression off the field as well, for example by acting violently toward women. A number of sociologists and women's advocates assert that because athletes are required to be aggressive, they commit acts of sexual violence at a higher rate than the general population. These experts point to research that indicates that both amateur and professional athletes are frequently charged with sexual assault. For instance, a 1994 study by researchers at Northeastern University and the University of Massachusetts at Amherst found that while male athletes made up 3.3 percent of the student population at ten large colleges, they represented 19 percent of the men charged with sexual assault on the campuses from 1991 to 1993. In addition, a survey by the *Washington Post* found that 141 professional and college football players in forty cities were charged with 156 offenses against women from January 1989 to November 1994. Critics argue that the approval of violent behavior that permeates many sports leads some athletes to act violently in other aspects of life, such as in their relationships with women.

Other commentators maintain, however, that more nonathletes than athletes are charged and convicted of sexual crimes. Athletes are perceived as committing more crimes than other men, they assert, because athletes are closely scrutinized by the media. Those who believe athletes are unfairly targeted cite statistics from the U.S. Department of Justice, which show that more than one million sexual attacks—including 35,000 rapes—were reported in 1992 and 1993. The number of athletes charged with sex crimes make up a very small percentage of those sexual attacks, these critics contend.

Whether or not sports contribute to sexual violence is unclear. But experts do agree that there is no single cause for such crimes. The authors in the following chapter discuss some of the factors that are believed to lead to sexual violence.

"Pornography stereotypes, demeans, dehumanizes, and makes all women vulnerable to . . . violence."

PORNOGRAPHY CAUSES SEXUAL VIOLENCE

R. Barri Flowers

In the following viewpoint, R. Barri Flowers argues that the very nature of pornography victimizes women since it portrays them being humiliated and maltreated and reduces them to objects to be used for men's sexual pleasure. Furthermore, numerous studies have found a definite correlation between pornography and sexual violence against women, he asserts. Pornography not only causes violence against women, Flowers contends, it also harms boys and men by giving them a one-dimensional view of women. Flowers is a criminologist, social scientist, and author of The Victimization and Exploitation of Women and Children, from which this viewpoint is taken.

As you read, consider the following questions:

1. According to the author, why is pornography here to stay?
2. What is pornography's message to men, in Flowers's opinion?
3. What were the key recommendations of the Attorney General's Commission on Pornography, according to Flowers?

From The Victimization and Exploitation of Women and Children: A Study of Physical, Mental, and Sexual Maltreatment in the United States by R. Barri Flowers. Copyright ©1994 by Ronald B. Flowers. Reprinted by permission of McFarland & Company, Inc., Publishers, Jefferson, NC 28640.

Women have long been exploited through pornographic films, videos, photographs, and literature. Such materials often portray women as the sexual objects of men, in sexually explicit terms, in bondage, and, increasingly, in sadistic and violent pornography. The upsurge in the quantity and variety of pornography available in the United States since the 1970s has left many psychologists and feminist groups associating pornography to a similar rise in rape, sexual assaults, battering, and other violent crimes against women. However, banning pornography in this country has proven to be an impossible task due to the complex issues associated with free-speech guarantees, censorship, and defining what constitutes pornography and obscenity. Anti-pornography statutes have been declared unconstitutional and it appears that pornography and its potential harmful effects with respect to women may be here to stay. . . .

THE BUSINESS OF PORNOGRAPHY

By most accounts, pornography is an enormous business in the United States, taking in an estimated $6 billion annually. The major players in the porn business include producers, distributors, advertisers, photographers, actors, and models. The sources for pornography are more diverse than ever before and include theaters, magazines, video stores, adult bookstores, cable television, and even network television where semi-nude women and violence against women have reached new levels, despite increased censorship and government regulations. Consequently, pornography consumers and viewers have an endless range of choices in the marketplace, meaning millions upon millions of dollars for the suppliers of pornographic materials, programming, live shows, etc.

By its very nature, pornography is an industry that has supported itself through "systematically eroticizing violence against women by producing and marketing images of men humiliating, battering, and murdering women for sexual pleasure. . . . Pornography is about power imbalances using sex as a weapon to subjugate women. In pornography the theme is assailant vs. victim," according to Frances Patai. The messages men receive from pornography's exploitation and victimization of women include the following:

- Women are passive, willing partners in their own victimization and exploitation.
- Women in pain are glamorous.
- Women are incapable of being independent or self-directed.
- It is appropriate that women's sexuality and behavior be

defined by men.
- Men are entitled to frequent, unconditional use of women's bodies for men's pleasure.

Patai, organizer of Women Against Pornography, argues that: "Pornography objectifies women by caricaturing and reducing them to a sum of their sexual parts and functions—devoid of sensibilities and intelligence."

THE COMMISSION ON PORNOGRAPHY

In 1985, the Attorney General's Commission on Pornography was established to "determine the nature, extent, and impact on society of pornography in the United States, and to make specific recommendations to the Attorney General concerning more effective ways in which the spread of pornography could be contained." A government Commission on Obscenity and Pornography in 1970 had found no link between pornography and violent crime against women.

The 11-member Attorney General's Commission concluded that there was a correlation between certain types of pornography and sexually violent and abusive crimes toward women, adding that exposure to even nonviolent sexually explicit material "bears some causal relationship to the level of sexual violence." The Commission's report read:

> When clinical and experimental research has focused particularly on sexually violent material, the conclusions have been nearly unanimous. In both clinical and experimental settings, exposure to sexually violent materials has indicated an increase in the likelihood of aggression. More specifically, the research . . . shows a causal relationship between exposure to material of this type and aggressive behavior towards women. . . . The assumption that increased aggressive behavior towards women is causally related, for an aggregate population, to increased sexual violence is significantly supported by the clinical evidence, as well as by much of the less scientific evidence.

The Commission called for a nationwide crackdown on the purveyors of hard-core pornography. Its key recommendations to Congress included:
- Amend the federal obscenity laws to eliminate the necessity of proving transportation to interstate commerce. A statute should be enacted only to require proof that distributing obscene material "affects" interstate commerce.
- Enact a forfeiture statute to reach the proceeds and instruments of any offense committed under the federal obscenity laws.

- Amend Title 18 of the United States Code to specifically pro-scribe obscene cable and satellite television programming.
- Enact legislation to make it an unfair business practice and an unfair labor practice for any employer to hire individu-als to participate in commercial sexual performances.
- Enact legislation prohibiting the transmission of obscene material through the telephone or similar common carrier.

Although the Attorney General's Commission on Pornography had its share of critics and criticism, the vast data used in the Commission's findings and recommendations "clearly justify the conclusion that there is at least some relationship between the pornography industry and the victimization of women," [Ronald B. Flowers, *Women and Criminality*, 1987].

PORNOGRAPHY AND BATTERED WOMEN

The link between pornography and woman battering has been increasingly established in the literature. In *Take Back the Night: Women on Pornography*, Laura Lederer asserts that "pornography is the ideology of a culture which promotes and condones rape, woman battering, and other crimes against women." The fol-lowing examples illustrate the association between pornography and the battering of women:

- In the movie *Swept Away*, an independent woman is system-atically verbally and physically abused until being reduced to a passive sexual subordinate who desires further humili-ation while loving her batterer.
- An album cover accentuates the crotch of a woman with the words: "Jump on It!"
- In the movie *Dressed to Kill*, women are portrayed as sex ob-jects and are raped, tortured, and murdered, though the crit-ics praised the film using such terms as "funny," "erotic," and "irresistible."

The co-editor of *Rape and Child Abuse* describes the relationship between battered women and pornography:

Woman battering objectifies women by reducing them to objects of possession. Both pornography and woman battering legitimize the pain inflicted on the woman by objectifying the woman. In addition, many women are raped and verbally assaulted while being battered. . . . Objectifying the sexual anatomy of women renders them inferior and nonhuman, thus providing the psy-chological foundation for committing violence against them.

Studies of battered women have established a correlation to pornography. A study of 100 abused wives by Kathleen Barry re-vealed that 15 percent of the women reported that their abusive spouses "seemed to experience sexual arousal from the violence—since the demand for sexual intercourse immediately followed the assault."

PORN TEACHES SEXUAL VIOLENCE

I believe there are many different causes of rape, and the significance of pornography varies depending on its availability, its content and the degree of its acceptability in a particular country. In nations saturated with porn, as the United States is, scientific evidence shows [that] pornography predisposes some men to want to rape women, and intensifies the predisposition in some other men already so predisposed.

For example, research has shown that porn combining sex and violence against women teaches some male viewers to be turned on by such violence.

Diana E.H. Russell, *On the Issues*, Summer 1995.

Pornography and its effects on wife batterers is still being studied. The evidence seems to support Patai's contention that "pornography (especially as it is legitimized in mainstream TV shows, ads, movies, fashion layouts, etc.) socializes some men into thinking that the maltreatment of women is erotic, sexually desirable, desired by women, and a necessary proof of virility."

PORNOGRAPHY AND SEXUAL ASSAULTS

Researchers have shown significant relationship between pornography and sex crimes. In a study of rape victims, sociologist Pauline Bart noted:

I didn't start out being against pornography; but if you're a rape researcher, it becomes clear that there is a direct link. Violent pornography is like an advertisement for rape. . . . Men are not born thinking women enjoy rape and torture. . . . They learn from pornography.

In a study of mass-circulation sex magazines and the incidence of rape, Larry Baron and Murray Straus found that "rape increases in direct proportion to the readership of sex magazines." Neil Malamuth, co-editor of *Pornography and Sexual Aggression*, warned that "in a culture that celebrates rape, the lives of millions of women will be affected."

Law enforcement data further bolster the link between pornography and sexual assault of women. Michigan police recently analyzed more than two decades of sex crimes in the state and found numerous cases where the assailants had immersed themselves in pornographic films or pictures and then gone out and committed sex crimes. These crimes included rape, sodomy, and even the bizarre erotic crime of piquerism (piercing with a knife till blood flows, a kind of sexual torture). In some cases, the attacker admitted that the urge to rape or torture erotically came over him while reading an obscene picture magazine or attending a movie showing rape and erotic torture.

The Los Angeles Police Department found a strong link between the clustering of adult entertainment establishments in Hollywood and an increase in the incidence of rape and other violent crimes. Pornography is also often associated with female prostitution. . . . The LAPD found that prostitution in the Hollywood adult entertainment district during a recent six-year period increased at a rate 15 times the city average.

Prostitution and pornography have also been shown to be related to sexual assaults and physical violence against female prostitutes, including murder.

PORNOGRAPHY AND THE EXPLOITATION OF WOMEN

Perhaps the greatest victimization women must endure from pornography is the exploitation it inflicts on women inside and outside the industry. Women in pornographic materials and shows are typically nude or scantily clad, vacuous, abused, degraded, manipulated, paid less than their male counterparts, rarely in upper level production or directorial positions, and used at the whim of and largely for the entertainment of men. The residual effect is that pornography stereotypes, demeans, dehumanizes, and makes all women vulnerable to misinterpretations, imagination, lasciviousness, salaciousness, and violence.

In *The Seduction of Society*, William Stanmeyer addresses the exploitation of women by pornographers:

Pornography feeds twisted male fantasies about women. Invariably the pornographic film or photo shows a beautiful woman vulnerable and available to be used, roughly, by the male with whom the viewer identifies. . . . The woman is made to appear no more than a function or an organ. The camera's focus and interest is solely genital: it is irrelevant who this person is; any woman would do, as long as her physical attributes are exaggerated. She has no value in herself, her only value and purpose is for the male. She is quite simply an object. She is a thing. This is true even if the pornography is not explicitly violent. Pornography that is not overtly violent is still implicitly violent because it objectifies and degrades women.

The danger of pornography and its effects are not only to

women but potentially to each of us, as the following passage from an article on pornography by Linda T. Sanford and Mary E. Donovan reveals:

> Pornography hurts all women by portraying them only as sexual objects. And it hurts men and boys as well, especially those who are exposed to pornography at an early age, by giving them a limited, leering view of women. In sum, pornography damages everyone in our society.

"Men who use force in their relations
with women have done so for
centuries before the camera [was
invented]."

PORNOGRAPHY DOES NOT CAUSE SEXUAL VIOLENCE

Marcia Pally

In the following viewpoint, Marcia Pally maintains that sexually
explicit material is not responsible for men's sexual violence
against women. Men rape because they want to inflict pain, she
asserts, not because they were exposed to pornography. Therefore, Pally contends, rapists who claim that pornography inspired their crimes are merely trying to rationalize or justify
their behavior. Pally is cofounder of Feminists for Free Expres-
sions, a nonprofit anticensorship organization, and the author of
Sense and Censorship: The Vanity of the Bonfires and *Sex and Sensibility: Reflections on Forbidden Mirrors and the Will to Censor*, from which this viewpoint is excerpted.

As you read, consider the following questions:
1. What is women's true problem, according to the author?
2. In Pally's opinion, why should sex offenders' claims that
   pornography was responsible for their actions be examined
   carefully?
3. What percentage of adult videotapes were rented by women
   in 1990 and 1991, according to Pally?

A popular argument against sexually explicit material, rap, and rock is that men get ideas from them and force women to do what the photos or lyrics depict. Yet it is not sex, the positions, or costumes, but force—economic, psychological, and physical—that is women's problem. Coercion is much older than rock or pornography. The most conservative image-blamers would not refute the history that men who use force in their relations with women have done so for centuries before the camera and compact disc, and not only in sex but in every area of life. With their focus on sex, image-blamers [those who blame pornography for sexual violence] leave the uncomfortable impression that they do not concern themselves with the wide array of nonsexual coercions. Women's intimidation begins not with the commercialized image but with confusion and powerlessness. Those who wish women well are wasting their time until they help them acquire the emotional means to know their desires and the economic means to say "no" not only to unwanted sex but to bullying and intimidation of all sorts.

TED BUNDY'S DEFENSE

Another popular support for censorship is the rapists and wife batterers who tell their court-appointed social workers that they learned their ways from pornography. Ted Bundy, on his deathbed, offered the public his conversion to this idea. It is a clever ploy; look at who gets off the hook. It is some measure of the Meese Commission's [the 1986 Attorney General's Commission on Pornography] thinking that Dr. Judith Becker and Ellen Levine felt constrained to write in their dissenting report, "Information from the sex-offender population must be interpreted with care because it may be self-serving." [Bundy is thought to have raped and murdered as many as fifty women in the 1970s.]

Dr. Gene Abel, professor of psychiatry, Emory University School of Medicine, said at the time of the Bundy execution in 1989, "What we find is that sex offenders have rationalizations and justifications for their behavior. And Ted Bundy, like most of the sadists we've dealt with, had a lot of false beliefs or rationalizations to explain his behavior. What he said, in essence, was, 'It isn't my fault, these are pornographic things that I've seen.' And we just don't see that relationship."

Dr. Emanuel Tanay, the psychiatrist who interviewed Bundy after his arrest in Florida, said, "Pornography doesn't have the power to cause the severe deformity of personality that he [Bundy] had." Bundy's lawyer, James Coleman, said of Bundy's final interview, "It was vintage Bundy. It was Bundy the actor. He didn't know what made him kill people. No one did."

According to Norma Wagner, director of the adult sexual offender program at South Florida State Hospital, "Pornography is probably more a symptom than a cause. Just as adolescent animal torture and arson are symptoms—not causes—of a personality that is likely to commit violent crimes, sexual or otherwise." Of the basic Bundy argument, Dr. Irwin Stotzky, professor of criminal law at the University of Miami, said, "The argument that looking at pornography will lead to violence is like saying alcohol advertisements will lead to heroin addiction."

A VIOLENT CHILDHOOD INFLUENCE

Dr. Dorothy Lewis, professor of psychiatry at New York University and clinical professor at Yale University Child Study Center, conducted multiple interviews with Bundy and his family after his arrest. She discovered that at age three, Bundy had begun such unusual rituals as sticking butcher knives into his bed. At the time, Bundy and his mother were living with Bundy's grandfather, who, according to family reports, beat and tortured animals, threw Bundy's aunt down a flight of stairs, and regularly terrorized family members. After repeated butcher-knife performances, the family felt that Bundy's grandfather so adversely affected the boy that he and his mother should be moved out of the house. Dr. Lewis diagnosed Bundy as suffering since 1967 from manic depressive psychosis, characterized by extreme mood changes including rage, euphoria, and depression.

When Bundy was arrested in 1978, he was found not with violent pornography but with magazines advertising cheerleader camps. In his early interviews, he referred to popular sexual magazines as "normal, healthy sexual stimuli," and admitted he was turned on by nonsexual fare. Only in the mid-'80s, when the court refused to declare Bundy insane and so remove the threat of capital punishment, did Bundy convert to born-again Christianity and begin collecting information attesting to the negative effects of pornography. By 1986, he was condemning popular soft-core magazines because they caused arousal for someone other than one's spouse.

In 1987, Bundy started quoting research by Edward Donnerstein and Daniel Linz that he hoped would bolster his pornography-made-me-do-it claim. He failed to include the authors' conclusion that in no study "has a measure of motivation such as 'likelihood to rape' ever changed as a result of exposure to pornography. . . . There is no reason to think that exposure to violent pornography is the cause of these predispositions [to rape]." In his final interview, Bundy said, "The FBI's own study on serial homicide shows that the most common interest among serial killers is pornography." The FBI makes no claim that pornography causes serial murder or other violent crime.

NO CAUSAL CONNECTION

A causal connection between exposure to pornography and the commission of sexual violence has never been established. The National Research Council's Panel on Understanding and Preventing Violence concluded in a 1993 survey of laboratory studies that "demonstrated empirical links between pornography and sex crimes in general are weak or absent." Even according to another research literature survey that former U.S. Surgeon General C. Everett Koop conducted at the behest of the staunchly anti-pornography Meese Commission, only two reliable generalizations could be made about the impact of "degrading" sexual material on its viewers: it caused them to think that a variety of sexual practices was more common than they had previously believed, and to more accurately estimate the prevalence of varied sexual practices.

Nadine Strossen, *Humanist*, May/June 1995.

Barry Lynn notes in the *Harvard Civil Rights–Civil Liberties Law Review* that criminals have confessed they were inspired by "the golden calf scene in Cecil B. DeMille's *The Ten Commandments* and an Anglican church service. For some defendants, of course, pornography has become a convenient excuse for their actions, an excuse more in tune with the times than blaming 'comic books' and more plausible than blaming Twinkies [as did Dan White, the convicted murderer of San Francisco mayor George Moscone and supervisor Harvey Milk]. . . . If a piece of feminist literature led even one man to respond with violence, should it too be regulated, under a theory that it caused him to feel threatened and triggered him to act out his aggression?"

REBUTTALS TO ANTIPORNOGRAPHY ARGUMENTS

Lynn's question might also be asked of those who propose that men rape because they learned—from pornography or rap—that it is acceptable or that women like it. There is something amiss with the idea that men harass and rape to *please* women, or to find favor with authority figures because harassment and rape are "acceptable." To the rapist facing his victim, it has always been clear that she did not "want it." The teenagers who in 1993 yanked the bathing suits off girls at swimming pools in

New York knew it was neither acceptable nor pleasurable. Men rape because it hurts and they do it to hurt women. If society wants to reduce rape, it must address the reasons why men want to inflict such pain.

Finally, one comes across the argument that nobody likes pornography and that communities have the right to rid themselves of the junk that nefarious and sleazy outsiders bring in. This is a fine argument that the marketplace briskly addresses. If material does not sell, shopkeepers will not stock it. If they reorder, someone is buying. The retrospective of Robert Mapplethorpe photographs earned the Cincinnati Contemporary Arts Center a record number of visitors and new museum members. A jury of local residents judged it fit for public exhibition. One wonders who was the community whose standards these photographs breached so severely that a museum and curator were taken to trial.

Image-blamers would have one believe that only unhealthy, troubled characters use sexual material, and certainly no women. From this they reason the women must be protected from it. The sales receipts of sexually explicit material tell a different story. Nineteen ninety-two saw $462 million in wholesale sales of adult videos and 445 million adult video rentals. The figures for 1991 were $395 million in wholesale sales and 410 million rentals. In the recession of 1989, $325 million were spent in wholesale sales and 395 million adult tapes were rented; in 1988, $390 million was spent wholesale and 398 million adult videotapes were rented. A conservative estimate would suggest two viewers per rental, making 800–900 million viewings per year. In 1990 and 1991, 47 percent of adult videotapes were rented by women in couples or women alone, a trend seen even in conservative southern states. In 1990, Jack Humphrey, manager of a chain of video outlets in Florida, reported that sales and rentals of adult tapes were up 85 percent between 1988 and 1990. "The biggest increase is in the number of women who come in," he said. "Now about 50% of our customers are women." Relying on traditional notions of female asexuality and "purity," image-blamers may be more sexist than the pornography they would ban.

> "Violent and demeaning musical lyrics have a deleterious effect on our youth."

RAP MUSIC PROMOTES SEXUAL VIOLENCE

Robert T.M. Phillips

Just as research shows that television violence desensitizes the viewer to real-life violence, so too do nihilistic and misogynistic music lyrics, according to Robert T.M. Phillips. In the following viewpoint, Phillips contends that the violent lyrics of rap music are especially worrisome because children, who have the innate desire to imitate behavior they see and hear, will be tempted to act out the sexually violent behavior depicted in the songs. Phillips is the deputy medical director of the American Psychiatric Association, a professional association of psychiatrists.

As you read, consider the following questions:

1. What percentage of violent crimes were committed by juveniles in 1991, according to Phillips?
2. What types of music other than rap contain violent lyrics, in the author's opinion?
3. According to Phillips, what attitudes were expressed by men who listened to heavy metal rock music?

From a statement on behalf of the American Psychiatric Association by Robert T.M. Phillips in *Shaping Our Responses to Violent and Demeaning Imagery in Popular Music*, a hearing before the U.S. Senate Judiciary Committee, Subcommittee on Juvenile Justice, 103rd Cong., 2nd sess., February 23, 1994.

We are a society that is infatuated with violence in a clinically obsessive way. We romanticize violence in film. We glorify violent sports and pay homage to its gladiators with adoration and attach to such sport the financial rewards and spoils of our society. We feed our addiction to violence in television news trailers for the five, six, ten, and eleven p.m. broadcasts. We sensationalize violence with special reports and special editions in both the electronic and print media. From Los Angeles to Lillehammer, violence has emerged as the strongest currency in a marketplace that just can't get enough.

VIOLENCE AND CHILDREN

Children have increasingly become not only the victims of violence, but also its fastest growing segment of perpetrators. Juveniles accounted for 17 percent of all violent crimes in calendar year 1991. The juvenile arrest rates for murder increased by 85 percent between the years 1987–1991. Three out of every ten juvenile murder arrests in this country involve a victim under the age of 18. There is no hope of getting violence off our streets until we figure out how to get the guns out of the hands of our young children. Between 1987 and 1991 the juvenile arrest rates for weapons violations increased by 62 percent. In 1991 one out of every five weapons arrests was a juvenile arrest. Most disturbing to me as an African-American psychiatrist is the fact that black youth were arrested for weapons law violations at a rate triple that of white youth in 1991. Black youth were the victims of homicide at a rate six times higher than whites.

Among our young today, in particular our minority young, anger, frustration, hopelessness, and rage fuel the fires that inevitably are manifested in violence. The compounding problems of substance abuse, teenage pregnancy, illiteracy, truancy and dropping out have provided fertile soil for the seeds of discontent that have been sown for generations in this country. The deterioration of the family unit and the absence of strong and consistent male and female role models only begin to help us understand the origins of this dilemma.

Much attention has been focused on the effects of violent television programming on children and adolescents. The American Psychiatric Association has joined with Senator Kent Conrad and the Citizens Task Force on TV Violence and is already on record regarding this issue. Now our attention appropriately turns to the recording industry and the impact of sexually explicit lyrics on the physical and emotional well-being of our young. If television and movies are the window through which we see the reflections of art imitating life, then music is clearly the homing device of language by which we track the cultures and mores of our society.

Numerous studies have clearly established the relationship between actual exposure to violence and its negative consequences on normal childhood development. A substantial body of research has also demonstrated the association of violent or aggressive behaviors with repeated exposure to televised violence. Simply put, the more violent programming children view, the greater is the risk that they will behave violently or aggressively.

NIHILISTIC AND PORNOGRAPHIC

The same paradigm holds true for music and its potential effect on listeners. Rock music has always been viewed as a "counter-culture" by many adults. Nonetheless, it has firmly established itself as a powerful art form, particularly among the young. As each generation matures, what was considered the "norm" becomes passe as new contemporary themes emerge. Recently, there has been an appropriate decrying of a form of rap music referred to as "gansta rap" whose lyrics contain some of the most violent and derogatory verbal assaults on women. We seem, however, to have forgotten that this is only the latest iteration of a theme which long predated rap music. Other forms of contemporary rock music, in particular certain segments of heavy metal and hard core punk, have persistently demonstrated substantial deviation, even from the "norm," of current contemporary themes. This type of music has been described by critics and researchers alike as "alienated, negativistic, nihilistic, and pornographic" at its best. A review of the lyrics of this kind of contemporary rock music reveals themes of homicide, suicide and satanic practices, which promote sex, sadomasochism, rape, and murder. There have also been clear examples in which lyrics have promoted the act of suicide. [A] review of adolescent interests in view of destructive themes in rock music provides us with some sample lyrics released since 1980 by heavy metal bands:

No apparent motive/Just kill and kill again/Survive my brutal slashing/I'll hunt you till the end
By Slayer

In goes my knife/Pull out his life/Consider that bastard dead
By Motley Crüe

Ripping flesh, drawing blood/I live to eat your bones
By Metal Church

I am possessed by all that is evil/The death of your God I de-mand/I spit at the virgin you worship/And sit at Lord Satan's right hand

By Venom

Holy hell, death to us/Satan fell, unholy lust/Devil's water starts to flood/God is slaughtered, drink his blood . . . Satan's right hand

By Seven Churches

A REPUGNANT EVOLUTION

The lyrics of "gansta rap" and misogyny in rap clearly then evolve from the same shameful and repugnant tradition.

So if you at a show in the front row
I'm a call you a bitch or a dirty-ass ho
You probably get mad like bitch is supposed to . . .
So what about the bitch who got shot?
F--- her
You think I give a damn about a bitch

By N.W.A.

Bitch . . . I just want f--- you and cut
Treat ya like a trammpy slut.

By Too Short

Her body's beautiful so I'm thinking rape
Shouldn't have had her curtains open so that's her fate . . .
Slit her throat and watched her shake

By The Ghetto Boys

Cause we're like the outlaws striding while suckers are hiding . . .
Jump behind the bush when you see me drivin' by!
Hanging out the window with my magnum taking out some putas. Act kind of local, I'm just another local kid from the street getting paid for my vocals.

By Cypress Hill

THE RESEARCH

The effect of such music and music videos is best understood in in the context of childhood development. Children are born with the innate capacity and desire to imitate adult human be-havior. Whether the behavior imitated is triggered by a visual image, an audio image, or by combined audio-visual imagery, the cognitive impact is overwhelming. Violence is powerful, tan-talizing, charismatic, and intoxicating.

Research on the impact of music and music videos on nor-mal child development has been consistent with similar research that has examined the impact of repeated exposure to televised violence.

Approximately 700 middle and high school students from central Florida completed a survey about rock music preferences. Nearly one-fifth of the students named as favorites those performers whose music describes homicide, suicide, and satanism. The majority of these fans were male. Among those studied, fans of heavy metal and punk rock were more likely than fans of other rock music to report knowing the lyrics to favorite songs.

PORNOGRAPHIC SMUT

I want to address the issue of the impact of gangster rap lyrics and images on the youth of America. The misogynist lyrics that glorify violence and denigrate women are nothing more than pornographic smut. This smut being sold to our children coerces, influences, encourages and motivates our youth to commit violent behavior, use drugs and abuse women through demeaning sex acts. Our youth's constant exposure to these menacing images lowers their sensibilities toward violent behavior, making killing and abuse commonplace and acceptable.

From C. DeLores Tucker's statement to the U.S. Senate Judiciary Committee's Subcommittee on Juvenile Justice, February 23, 1994.

A content analysis of music videos was conducted by the Journal of Broadcasting & Electronic Media. The study found that violence and crime were depicted in more than half of a random sample of 62 music videos shown on MTV. Violent videos featured destruction of property, physical aggression against self and others, and use of weapons such as chains, guns, knives and axes.

The effects of sexually violent rock music on men's acceptance of violence against women was reported in Psychology of Women Quarterly. Seventy-five male college students participated in an experiment to compare the effects of exposure to sexually violent heavy metal rock, Christian heavy metal rock, and easy-listening music on attitudes about women. The study found that men who listened to only seventeen minutes of heavy metal music (regardless of sexually violent or Christian themes) expressed greater endorsement of sexual stereotypes, negative attitudes and prejudicial beliefs about women than did men who heard easy-listening music. . . .

These data are clear, convincing and overwhelming. The repeated exposure to violent imagery desensitizes us to violence and greatly increases the risk that we will manifest violence in our own behavior. We must educate parents to the risks of exposure to such music in the same way we have educated them to the risks of exposure to infectious diseases.

Freedom of speech does not relieve artists, recording executives, or broadcasters of their responsibility to serve the public interest. More importantly, one's constitutionally guaranteed First Amendment right to free speech does not give license to do harm to others.

The American Psychiatric Association believes that violent and demeaning musical lyrics have a deleterious effect on our youth and place at grave risk the mental health and welfare of themselves and our communities.

| "[Hip-hop music] doesn't cause violence, any more than preaching about adultery causes adultery."

RAP MUSIC DOES NOT PROMOTE SEXUAL VIOLENCE

Harry Allen

Harry Allen is a columnist with the periodical City Sun in New York City and the director of "enemy relations" for the rap group Public Enemy. In the following viewpoint, Allen contends that rap music is not responsible for violence in the black community. Rather than causing violence, Allen maintains, rap music gives blacks a method of expressing and criticizing the violence and racism they experience in their lives every day.

As you read, consider the following questions:

1. What evidence does the author present to support his contention that alcohol is responsible for violence against blacks?
2. What is the number one problem for blacks, according to Allen?
3. In the author's opinion, what is necessary to eliminate blacks' problems?

If the Black people who manage Inner City Broadcasting (owners of radio station WBLS in New York), radio station KACE in Los Angeles, and other urban media companies are so interested in protecting their listening audiences from violence, misogyny and profanity—as they should be, and as they recently said they were when they banned certain songs—why do they still accept advertising from liquor manufacturers, especially malt-liquor advertising, and promote these products for money?

ALCOHOL AND VIOLENCE

"Violence"? The use of the drug alcohol has been scientifically and significantly connected to a host of ills that plague Black people: murder; job absenteeism and unemployment; low birth weight; abnormalities and retardation in infants; liver and heart disease; poor academic performance; fires; homelessness; as well as rising incidences of cancer and AIDS. More than 18 million U.S. adults have significant alcohol-related problems. Twenty percent of all hospital costs, 46,000 traffic-crash deaths and 534,000 injuries annually, one-third of all drowning and boat deaths, 54 percent of all people convicted of violent crimes, 20 to 36 percent of all suicides, and the majority of rapes and assaults in the United States are *directly alcohol-related*.

"Misogyny" and "profanity"? Though program directors might find no official statistics to verify this, ask female members of your audience how high the "---- you, bitch!"-count goes after their mate drinks a high-alcohol "G. Heileman Brewing Co., La Crosse, Wisconsin," product. You know—like Colt 45. Ask how many have gotten hit after their man took a hit from one of your most lucrative advertisers' products. Then reread the U.S. Department of Health and Human Services, U.S. Department of Justice, U.S. Department of Transportation, Census Bureau and Centers for Disease Control figures cited above, and weep. The social costs of alcohol-related problems are more than $85 billion and 105,000 deaths per year. That's nearly twice the number of "Americans" who died in Vietnam.

Also, please don't give us that "our product, when used in moderation" line, either. Approximately $1 of social costs is created for *every retail dollar spent* on alcoholic beverages. In other words, this stuff is literally *useless*.

Meanwhile, the use of hip-hop has been scientifically connected to . . . well, nothing but the use of hip-hop. So whom in the world are Black media people really trying to protect? Their audience? Or their stations' low ratings, low shares and wealthy, white big-ticket-item advertisers, especially the ones who pay more for an adult Black audience than they do for the Black teenage one that hip-hop draws?

In 1994, a lot of the best-dressed, best-educated, best-spoken, most religious Black people gave quality time to attacking hip-hop. Call it giving out placebos for poison, or putting a Band-Aid on a bullet wound. If you run down the list of Black people's top 100 problems, "gangsta rap"—a vague and undefined musical category—places somewhere around 439th.

A BALANCED MIX

Rap isn't—and never was—a monolithic style. Critics contend that rap is racist, violent, and sexist; slapping those labels on the entire genre makes as little sense as denouncing all rock music when Axl Rose gets in a fistfight. The highly competitive nature of rap has actually encouraged a much greater balance of voices than any other type of pop music. "Gangsta" rappers like Ice-T and N.W.A. (Niggas with Attitude) write vicious lyrics peppered with obscenity, while Ed O.G & DA Bulldogs counsel young men to be responsible fathers. The raunchy, funny, and extremely sexist rhymes of 2 Live Crew find their match with the raunchy, funny, and extremely feminist rhymes of Bytches with Problems or the proud, clean-cut lyrics of Queen Latifah. Other performers expound on such diverse topics as love, politics, education, Hispanic pride, and life in the suburbs.

Michael Small, *Vogue*, March 1993.

White supremacy is No. 1 with a bullet. White supremacy is the phenomenon to which hip-hop is itself a reaction. But none of the Black people publicly criticizing hip-hop, or "certain kinds of rap music," have, at the same time, provided a succinct analysis of the white-supremacy phenomenon. None has even mentioned white supremacy by name. Why is that?

In the meantime, hip-hop rockets in influence.

PERSUASIVE AND RELEVANT

Why? Because it is an artistically adventurous culture that makes a robust—one would even say an obvious—criticism of racism, and racism's uncompensated insult. Because hip-hop is a wide and flexible form of communication that white record company and media executives, often criticized in the above scenarios, have shown great imagination in manipulating—imagination that Black people have not even begun to emulate.

Why? Because hip-hop is real-time; up-to-the-minute, high-band-width. This is how it works: The vocalists—those who dramatize violence on their records and those who don't—take the things that Black people *see*, *talk* about them and, in doing so, make those things *rhythmic*. Doing this, then, makes those things, for Black people, *persuasive* and *relevant*. Hip-hop is really a form of *preaching*.

THE ROOT CAUSE OF VIOLENCE

This process doesn't *cause* violence, any more than preaching about adultery causes adultery. This process is caused *by* violence. It is preceded by centuries of white-on-Black violence that Black people have yet to fully *mention*, even as we inherit this legacy. I mean, really: If *you* were going to make a song about an existence where the midnight sounds of automatic gunfire riddled your dreams, what would you call that song? "Betcha by Golly Wow"? "Sketches of Spain"? "Mr. Sandman"?

Or would you call it "Trigga Gots No Heart"? Hip-hop, says Chuck D, is "Black people's CNN." Is that why so many people keep trying to turn it off? Just like with CNN, all of the "experts" thought hip-hop wasn't going to last, either.

We are not arguing for violence. No person should be violent except, perhaps, to stop violence. We are not arguing for Black people calling each other "bitches," "hoes," "niggers" or "niggas." No one should call any person a name that that person doesn't want to be called.

However, what we are arguing for is truth. That, and *consistency*. If you want to eliminate Black people's ills, you first must eliminate the root cause—racism, the sole expression of which is white supremacy. Much as ministers, politicians and regular folk try to get around it, there is no way past this obvious and glaring fact.

WHAT SHOULD BE DONE

If you don't want a low Arbitron rating, play what your audiences want to hear *when* they want to hear it, and not 15 *years* after a recorded music form starts!

If you don't want to promote violence, misogyny and profanity—all three—don't take ads for the "Beverly Hills Cop III" movie.

And if Black media people are against the things that they think *might* harm people ("gangsta rap," "quote-unquote-unquote-unquote"), why do they take money for pushing beer, malt liquor and wine, which *definitely* do? And if alcohol is a drug, why doesn't this make those Black media people *drug dealers?*

Yet, still, they are our mothers, fathers, uncles, aunts, brothers, sisters and friends. Hip-hop needs their knowledge and the benefit of their experience.

The problem, though, is that what hip-hop gets most consistently from older, "middle-class" Black people in "media," "management," "the public sector" and "the clergy" is criticism. Criticism. That, and a stifling, *stupefying* lack of vision.

"*All forms of female brutalization
. . . are but an exaggeration of the
male dominance and the female
objectification that have come to
seem normal and natural.*"

TRADITIONAL MALE/FEMALES ROLES PROMOTE SEXUAL VIOLENCE

Sandra Lipsitz Bem

Sandra Lipsitz Bem is a professor of psychology and women's studies at Cornell University. In the following viewpoint, which is excerpted from her book *The Lenses of Gender: Transforming the Debate on Sexual Inequality*, Bem argues that violence against women is the inevitable result of a society that is androcentric—centered around men. She maintains that men are expected to dominate women in every way—physically, emotionally, and sexually—and women are expected to satisfy men's needs and desires. Therefore, she contends, sexual violence is merely an exaggeration of the traditional sex roles. Nor is it surprising, Bem contends, to find that such violations are a frequent occurrence and that they are sexually exciting for men.

As you read, consider the following questions:

1. What is the conventional wisdom about sexual violence against women, according to the author?
2. How is sexual inequality eroticized by American society, in Bem's opinion?
3. According to Bem, why is a nude male body considered pornographic?

In recent years, an increasing number of Americans have finally begun to acknowledge the epidemic of male violence against women, which feminists have been insistently calling to everyone's attention ever since Susan Brownmiller published *Against Our Will* in 1975. Although the conventional wisdom conceptualizes such violence as the pathological product of a criminal or demented mind, what follows logically from feminist analysis in general . . . is that all forms of female brutalization—including rape and wife beating—are but an exaggeration of the male dominance and the female objectification that have come to seem normal and natural in the context of everyday heterosexuality. Put somewhat differently, the everyday way of experiencing heterosexual desire is itself so shaped by the androcentric and gender-polarizing conception of male dominance as normal and natural, and anything other than male dominance as alien and problematic, that the sexual brutalization of a woman by a man is not just an isolated act, a case of an individual man taking out his psychological problems on an individual woman. It is rather the inevitable cultural by-product of an androcentric heterosexuality that eroticizes sexual inequality.

MALE DOMINATION

This eroticizing of sexual inequality can be seen in what most Americans think of as perfectly normal and natural heterosexuality. First, although neither women nor men in American society tend to like heterosexual relationships in which the woman is bigger, taller, stronger, older, smarter, higher in status, more experienced, more educated, more talented, more confident, or more highly paid than the man, they do tend to like heterosexual relationships in which the man is bigger, taller, stronger, and so forth, than the woman.

Second, both women and men see it as normal and natural for the male to play a more dominant or assertive role in a heterosexual encounter and for the female to play a more yielding or accommodating role. They also see it as emasculating for the man and defeminizing for the woman if those assertive and yielding roles are reversed on a regular basis. In normal, everyday heterosexual eroticism, the male is thus supposed to be superior in a wide variety of personal characteristics related to status and to play the dominant role in virtually every aspect of the heterosexual encounter from initiating the date to arranging and paying for the entertainment to guiding the sexual activity.

Finally, both women and men see the female in general and the female body in particular as more the object of male sexual desire than as a desiring sexual subject (or agent). This objectification, which manifests itself in the extraordinary emphasis on a woman's physical attractiveness in American culture, as well as in the almost continuous display of the nude or seminude female body in art, advertising, and the mass media, constitutes an eroticizing of sexual inequality—as opposed to merely a celebrating of female sexuality—because it implicitly imposes a male perspective on the definition of female sexuality. It androcentrically defines women—and predisposes women to define themselves—not in terms of their own sexual desires but in terms of their ability to stimulate and satisfy the male's sexual desires.

"You seldom see such traditional family values these days."

Pepper . . . and Salt, from the *Wall Street Journal*; permission, Cartoon Features Syndicate

It is no accident that American culture has no comparable tradition of displaying the nude or seminude male body. The culture has so completely constructed females and nudes as the objects of male sexual desire that when Americans see a display of a nude or a seminude male body, they instantly assume that it is not a heterosexual woman's object of desire but a gay man's object of desire. This perception, in turn, so arouses their abhorrence of homosexuality that they end up judging the display of the nude male body itself as inherently pornographic.

DATE RAPE

Given how thoroughly embedded male dominance and female objectification are in even these three "normal" and taken-for-granted aspects of heterosexual desire, it follows that date rape would be a frequent occurrence. After all, when looking through androcentric and gender-polarizing lenses, the man finds it normal and natural to keep pushing for sex even when the woman is resisting a bit, and the woman finds it alien and problematic to assert herself so forcefully and unmistakably that the man will have no choice but to stop what he's doing or use force. Now, however, the norm is so much for men to keep making sexual advances and for women to keep resisting those advances without making a scene or even being impolite that many date rapists do not perceive the sexual intercourse they manage to get as an act of rape.

And if the frequency of date rape is not surprising, given the gender lenses that men and women wear, nor should it be surprising that so many men in American society find violence against women to be so sexually arousing, so affirming of their masculinity, or both, that they brutalize women directly or participate in such brutalization vicariously through violent pornography.

> "Men batter because we have been
> trained to; because there are few
> social sanctions against it; because
> . . . the exploitation of people . . . is
> acceptable."

SOCIETY TEACHES MEN TO BE VIOLENT

Robert L. Allen and Paul Kivel

Boys are taught from an early age by their parents and society that fighting is an acceptable way to solve a problem, maintain Robert L. Allen and Paul Kivel in the following viewpoint. Men are also taught to treat women as sexual objects, the authors contend. So it seems natural to males, Allen and Kivel argue, to prove their masculinity or take out their frustrations by hurting someone weaker, usually a female. Allen is a board member of the Oakland Men's Project, an organization dedicated to eradicating male violence, racism, and homophobia, and senior editor of the *Black Scholar* journal. Kivel is a cofounder of the Oakland Men's Project and author of *Men's Work: How to Stop the Violence That Tears Our Lives Apart*.

As you read, consider the following questions:

1. According to Allen and Kivel, what traits do boys feel they must exhibit in order to be considered "real men"?
2. What is the "Act Like a Man" box, according to the authors?
3. How do Allen and Kivel teach men to take responsibility for their violent actions?

W hy do men batter women? We have to discard the easy answers. Portraying batterers as ogres only serves to separate "them" from "us." But men who batter and men who don't are not all that different. Male violence is normal in our society and vast numbers of men participate. Men batter because we have been trained to; because there are few social sanctions against it; because we live in a society where the exploitation of people with less social and personal power is acceptable. In a patriarchal society, boys are taught to accept violence as a manly response to real or imagined threats, but they get little training in negotiating intimate relationships. And all too many men believe that they have the right to control or expect certain behavior from "their" women and children; many view difficulties in family relationships as a threat to their manhood, and they respond with violence.

Society's Role

Young people's definitions of femininity and masculinity often reflect rigid expectations of what they must live up to in order to be a "real" woman or a "real" man. Time and again we hear boys say that they are supposed to be tough, aggressive, in control, that they are not to express any feelings except anger, not to cry, and never to ask for help. And many boys expect girls to acquiesce to men and be dependent on them.

How do boys get these ideas about male identity and manhood? Often from parents, but our whole society contributes to the process. As many as one of every six boys are sexually assaulted, and many, many more are hit, yelled at, teased, and goaded into fighting to prove they're tough. At the Oakland Men's Project [an organization devoted to eradicating male violence, racism, and homophobia], we believe that many boys become convinced that they will be violated until they learn to use force to protect themselves. Then they move to take their pain and anger out on others the way older males have done to them.

In our work we often use role play as a way of getting at some of these issues. One particularly effective exercise involves a ten-year-old and his father: the father arrives home from work and demands that the boy turn off the TV, then berates him for the messiness of his room. The boy tries to explain; the father tells him to shut up, to stop making excuses. Fueling the father's anger is the fact that he's disappointed by the boy's school report card. The father shoves the report card in his son's face and demands to know why he has gotten a "D" in math. The boy says he did his best. The father tells him that he is stupid. The boy protests and begins to stand up. The father shoves him down, saying. "Don't you dare get up in my face!" The boy is visibly upset, and begins to cry. The father explodes: "Now what? You little mama's boy! You sissy! You make me sick. When are you going to grow up and start acting like a man?"

When we do this exercise in schools, it gets the boys' undivided attention because most have experienced being humiliated by an older male. Indeed, the power of this exercise is that it is so familiar. When asked what they learned from such encounters, the boys often say things like: A man is tough. A man is in control. A man doesn't cry. A man doesn't take crap.

SEXUAL IRRESPONSIBILITY

America's descent into violence and despair will continue until men rediscover the importance of personal responsibility, marital fidelity, and the meaning of love, Archbishop J. Francis Stafford declared in an interview published in the *Rocky Mountain News* on Sunday, December 6, 1993. . . .

The only way the violence can be stemmed, he said, is for society to insist on male sexual responsibility, but, he complained, "American society seems incapable or unwilling to take responsibility for men's sexuality. We are unwilling to say that fidelity, faithfulness to the mother of one's children, is inherent in what it means to be human."

Wanderer, December 16, 1993.

We write the boys' comments on a blackboard, draw a box around them, and label it the "Act Like a Man" box. We talk about how males in this culture are socialized to stay in the box. Eventually we ask: What happens if you step out of it, if you stop acting tough enough or man enough? Invariably we hear that you get called names like "fag," "queer," "mama's boy," "punk," "girl." Asked why, the boys say it's a challenge, that they're expected to fight to prove themselves. Homophobia and fear of being identified with women are powerful messages boys get from an early age, and they are expected to fight to prove that they're tough and not gay—that they're in the box.

Using exercises, like the father/son interchange, helps us examine how the male sex role often sets men up to be dominating, controlling, and abusive. We ask: How safe is it to stay in the "Act Like a Man" box? Usually, most admit that it isn't safe, because boys and men continually challenge each other to prove that they're in the box. When a boy or man is challenged, he can prove he's a man either by fighting the challenger or by finding someone "weaker"—a female or a more vulnerable male—to dominate. Hurting girls relieves any anxiety that we may not be tough enough and establishes our heterosexual credentials. It's both a sign of our interest (we're paying attention to them) and a symbol of our difference (we're in control).

THE UNSPOKEN CONTRACT

Because we are taught that women are primarily sexual objects, this behavior seems perfectly natural. And many men come to believe that a woman is just another material possession. We initiate dates, pay for our time together, protect them on the streets, and often marry them. We are trained to think that in return, girls should show their appreciation by taking care of us emotionally, putting their own concerns and interests aside, and putting out sexually.

This unspoken contract is one that many heterosexual men operate by, and it often leads to the assumption that women are our dumping grounds. If we've had a hard day at work, were embarrassed or humiliated by a boss—challenged in the box—the contract leads us to believe that we can take those feelings out on "our" women, and thus regain our power. If we end up hitting her, then we have to blame her in order to deny our aggression and keep our self-esteem intact. So we say things like: She asked for it. She pushed my buttons. She deserved it.

Invariably it comes as a surprise to us that women don't meekly accept our violence. So we respond by minimizing and justifying our actions: I didn't mean it. You're too sensitive. That's the way guys are. It was just the heat of the moment.

GETTING MEN TO TAKE RESPONSIBILITY

In order to get men to take responsibility for their own actions, we have to get them to talk about what they did, and what they said, and what they felt. Making the connection between how they have been trained and hurt and how they have learned to pass that pain on by hurting women or young people is essential.

To get men to reflect on their experiences and behaviors, we use exercises we call "stand ups." We ask everyone to be silent, and then slowly pose a series of questions or statements, and ask men to stand every time one applies to them. For example, we may ask, Have you ever:
- worried you were not tough enough?
- been called a wimp, queer, or fag?
- been told to "act like a man"?

- been hit by an older man?
- been forced to fight?
- been physically injured and hid the pain?
- been sexually abused, or touched in a way you didn't like?
- used alcohol or drugs to hide your pain?
- felt like blowing yourself away?

Later in the workshop we ask, Have you ever:
- interrupted a woman by talking louder?
- made a comment in public about a woman's body?
- discussed a woman's body with another man?
- been told by a woman that she wanted more affection and less sex from you?
- used your voice or body to intimidate a woman?
- hit, slapped, shoved, or pushed a woman?
- had sex with a woman when you knew she didn't want to?

Each participant is asked to look around and see other men standing, which helps break down their sense of isolation and feelings of shame. Since we are not a therapy group, no one is questioned or confronted about his own experiences. All of our work involves challenging the notion that males are naturally abusive and that females are natural targets of male abuse. We give boys and men a way of analyzing social roles by drawing insights from their own experiences, and help them to recognize that social interactions involve making choices, that we can break free of old roles by supporting each other in choosing alternatives to violence.

POWER AND VIOLENCE

An important part of our work is getting men and boys to look at how power, inequality, and the ability to do violence to others are structured into social relationships in this country. We discuss how these inequalities are maintained and how violence against one targeted group encourages violence against others. This is not to excuse men's behavior; it is done in the belief that in order to make better choices, men must understand the framework of power and violence that constantly pressures us to be in control and on top.

There are growing numbers of men who are critical of sexism. All too often they are isolated and fearful of raising their concerns with other men because they worry about being targeted for violence. We try to help them break through the fear and reach out to other men. But we also work to get men to understand how they are damaged by sexism and how male violence against women keeps us from the collective action needed to confront racial, gender-based, and economic injustice.

For us personally this is powerful, life-changing work. We were each drawn to it because of troubling issues in our own lives: issues around our relationships with our fathers (one emotionally abusive, the other emotionally distant); relationships with women partners where we found ourselves repeating controlling, sexist behaviors that made us feel guilty, ashamed, defensive; and the fear that we might do to our children what had been done to us as children. Through the work we have discovered that many men share these concerns, but they are hesitant to talk about this with other men. Sadly, we have all learned that "real" men don't admit vulnerability. But despite their initial hesitation, many men are eager to talk about their lives, and to change the controlling and abusive behavior they've been trained to pass on. Doing this work is healing for us and for those we work with.

MEN ARE RESPONSIBLE

Men are responsible for battery and for stopping male violence. If we are to counter the myth that men's abuse of women is natural, men must challenge each other to stop the violence. We must defy notions of manhood that lead us to injure or kill those we say we love. We must confront male friends when we see them heading down the destructive path of domestic violence and urge them to get help. While it is critical that domestic violence cases be taken more seriously by the police and criminal justice system, it is equally important to examine and to change underlying social attitudes and practices that promote and excuse domestic violence. This is truly men's work.

| "Rape has always been a military tactic, *a combat 'perk,' whether by* direct order or implicit prerogative."

RAPE IS FREQUENTLY USED AS A WEAPON OF WAR

Robin Morgan

The rape of Bosnian Muslim women in the early 1990s by Serbian soldiers was not an isolated case of rape being used in war, asserts Robin Morgan in the following viewpoint. Rape has been used as a weapon in war since the founding of Rome, she maintains. Morgan contends that invading armies use rape as a weapon to destroy a people's culture, heritage, and ethnicity. In such cases, according to Morgan, rape is a political act of torture. Morgan is the international consulting editor and former editor in chief of *Ms.* magazine.

As you read, consider the following questions:

1. How many women have been raped in the former Yugoslavia, according to the author?
2. What evidence does Morgan present to support her contention that the rape of Bosnian women is not an isolated incident?
3. How are the rapes in Bosnia unique, in Morgan's opinion?

F inally, the world believes it.

   Estimates differ, but as of April 1993, it was thought that 20,000 to possibly more than 50,000 women and girls in the former Yugoslavia have been raped, and countless others killed. Although the overwhelming number of rapes and forced pregnancies appear to have been committed by Serbian men against Bosnian Muslim women, men of all the opposing sides—Serbian, Croatian, and Bosnian Muslim—have apparently raped "each other's" women. That is the point: women are mere envelopes to carry the message of conquest from one group of men to another.

NOT AN ISOLATED INCIDENT

Finally the world believes it—but still doesn't make the connections. Instead, it chooses to regard this atrocity as an isolated incident, much as the Montreal Massacre was perceived as an aberration rather than an extreme expression of the "normal" climate of terror and violence female human beings everywhere endure. [In December 1989, fourteen female students were killed and thirteen others wounded at the University of Montreal by Marc Lepine, who blamed feminists for his failures.]

In Somalia in 1993, men of one warring clan raped women of another. There were also reports of harassment by coalition forces there; to compound the horror, religious fundamentalists were blaming the women. In January, four women were stoned to death and a fifth lashed 100 times as punishments for "prostitution." Another Somali woman remained in prison, facing a possible death sentence for the same charge, because she sought the protection of some French soldiers. . . .

An aberration? "Rape and take spoil" is an ancient motto of war. An isolated incident? Then what happened to the Sabine women? What did Alexander's armies do? Caesar's legions? The conquistadors and all the other colonizers? What of Chaka's Zulu army? The rape of Belgian and French women by German troops during World War I? What did their sons do to Russian women in World War II—and what did Russian troops do to German women "in response"? What about the institutionalized concentration-camp brothels where Jewish women were forced to supply "Enjoyment Duty" to their Nazi captors? The thousands of Chinese, Korean, and Filipina women conscripted into sexual slavery as "comfort women" for the Japanese army? The Chinese city where that army's actions were so extreme historians termed it "the Rape of Nanking"? The virtually ignored mass rape of Bengali women (estimated as high as 400,000)

during the 1971 Bangladesh-Pakistan war? What about Vietnam?
The Iraqi rapes of Kuwaiti women—and their Asian servants?

THE FIRST OPEN POLICY OF RAPE

If Bosnia is unique, it is because this may be the first time mass
rape and forced pregnancy have been used openly as a policy toward genocidal ends: the terrain is "ethnically cleansed" because
victims die and survivors flee, wishing never to return. And
what of the woman unable to get an abortion or find a home
for the product of rape? Five, ten years from now, when the
world has forgotten, will she have finally taught herself not to
read the torturer's features on the face of her child?

MASS RAPE'S DESTRUCTION

Alas for women, there is nothing unprecedented about mass
rape in war when enemy soldiers advance swiftly through popu-
lous regions, nor is it a precedent when, howling in misery,
leaders of the overrun country call the endemic sexual violence a
conspiracy to destroy their national pride, their manhood, their
honor. When German soldiers marched through Belgium in the
first months of World War I, rape was so extensive, and the
Franco-Belgian propaganda machine so deft, that The Rape of
the Hun became a ruling metaphor. . . .

Women are raped in war by ordinary youths as casually, or as fre-
netically, as a village is looted or gratuitously destroyed. Sexual
trespass on the enemy's women is one of the satisfactions of conquest, like a boot in the face, for once he is handed a rifle and
told to kill, the soldier becomes an adrenaline-rushed young man
with permission to kick in the door, to grab, to steal, to give vent
to his submerged rage against all women *who belong to other men.*

Sexual sadism arises with astonishing rapidity in ground warfare, when the penis becomes justified as a weapon in a logisti-
cal reality of unarmed noncombatants, encircled and trapped.
Rape of a doubly dehumanized object—as woman, as enemy—
carries its own terrible logic. In one act of aggression, the collective spirit of women *and* of the nation is broken, leaving a re-
minder long after the troops depart. And if she survives the assault, what does the victim of wartime rape become to her
people? Evidence of the enemy's bestiality. Symbol of her nation's defeat. A pariah. Damaged property. A pawn in the subtle
wars of international propaganda.

Susan Brownmiller, *Newsweek*, January 4, 1993.

Already we hear of captured Serbian soldiers claiming they
were commanded to rape against their will. Is this to lay the

ground for a war-crimes defense? Will the world remember that the phrase "I was only obeying orders" is an unacceptable defense for committing atrocities? Or is it different when only women suffer?

Rape has always been a military tactic, a combat "perk," whether by direct order or implicit prerogative. In 1992, when the U.N. Transitional Authority in Cambodia (UNTAC) received protests about the troops' behavior, UNTAC chief Yasushi Akashi replied that "18-year-old, hot-blooded soldiers" have a right to drink and chase "young, beautiful beings of the opposite sex." *Rape in war has always been a weapon*—one that should be as expressly forbidden in international law as chemical weapons and germ warfare. *Rape has always been an act of torment*, though it was not until 1991 that Amnesty International recognized rape as sex-specific torture. Rape is a violent act—and a political act. *How long must we scream to make the world understand?*

AN ACT OF HATE

Some honorable men who abhor the Bosnian tragedy still minimize rape in their own countries. Yet what is a "bias rape" but an "ethnic cleansing" sexual assault across racist lines? Some term this "hate rape"—a misnomer, since every rape is an act of hate. And what is the alleged gang-rape of a mentally disabled young woman in New Jersey in March 1989, if not a different form of bias rape?

"Animals," the columnists mutter, ignoring Hannah Arendt's warning about the banality of evil. Animals don't rape; men do. *If rape in war is a weapon, then what is it in peacetime?*

PERIODICAL BIBLIOGRAPHY

The following articles have been selected to supplement the diverse views presented in this chapter. Addresses are provided for periodicals not indexed in the *Readers' Guide to Periodical Literature*, the *Alternative Press Index*, the *Social Sciences Index*, or the *Index to Legal Periodicals and Books*.

Michael Albert	"Mackinnon?" *Z Magazine*, November 1993.
Ann Louise Bardach	"All in the Name of Islam," *Reader's Digest*, January 1994.
Walter Berns	"Learning to Live with Sex and Violence," *National Review*, November 1, 1993.
Bill Brubaker	"Violence off the Field," *Washington Post National Weekly Edition*, November 21–27, 1994. Available from Reprints, 1150 15th St. NW, Washington, DC 20071.
Kevin Chappell	"What's Wrong (and Right) About Black Music," *Ebony*, September 1995.
Wes Goodman	"Pornography, Peep Shows, and the Decline of Morality," *USA Today*, March 1994.
Laurence Jarvik	"Violence in Pursuit of Justice Is No Vice," *Insight*, December 19, 1994. Available from 3600 New York Ave. NE, Washington, DC 20002.
David McCabe	"Not-So-Strange Bedfellows," *In These Times*, March 7, 1994.
Lance Morrow	"Unspeakable," *Time*, February 22, 1993.
Marcia Pally	"The Great Soothing Appeal of Censorship," *Z Papers*, July–September 1994.
Laura Pitter and Alexandra Stiglmayer	"Will the World Remember? Can the Women Forget?" *Ms.*, March/April 1993.
Tara Roberts	"A Hip-Hop Nation Divided: Dilemma of a Womanist," *Essence*, August 1994.
Diana E. H. Russell	"Nadine Strossen: The Pornography Industry's Wet Dream," *On the Issues*, Summer 1995.
Chi Chi Sileo	"Are Rapists on Pleasure or Power Trips?" *Insight*, September 5, 1994.
Michael Small	"Rap's Bad Rap," *Vogue*, March 1993.
Nadine Strossen	"The Perils of Pornography," *Humanist*, May/June 1995.

CHAPTER 2

HOW SERIOUS A PROBLEM IS SEXUAL VIOLENCE?

CHAPTER PREFACE

Susan, a twenty-three-year-old student, went to answer a knock at her door and found a man she knew from one of her afternoon college courses. When she opened the door to let him in, he overpowered her, threw her on the couch, and raped her.

According to researcher Mary P. Koss, incidents like the above are more common than is generally reported. In a national sample of college students, for example, Koss and her colleagues discovered that 15 percent of women respondents had been raped, while an additional 12 percent had experienced attempted rape. These findings, Koss asserts, mean that at least one out of every four college women is a victim of rape or attempted rape. In another widely cited study, researcher Diana E.H. Russell interviewed a random sample of 930 San Francisco women about their lifetime experiences with physical and sexual violence. The results of this study led Russell to suggest that "at least 46 percent of American women will be victims of rape or attempted rape at some time in their lives." Furthermore, these researchers contend, most incidents of sexual violence against women are perpetrated by partners, relatives, or acquaintances of the victim. Rape appears to be "a common experience in women's lives," concludes Koss.

Other researchers dispute the findings of Russell, Koss, and their colleagues. University of California professor Neil Gilbert, for instance, argues that Koss's study uses an overly broad definition of rape. He points out that "if a woman said that she had had sexual intercourse when she did not want to, because a man gave her alcohol or drugs, Koss would label her a victim of rape." Gilbert believes that this definition of rape does not take into account whether or not the woman expressed lack of consent. Furthermore, Gilbert states, "seventy-three percent of those whom [Koss] defined as having been raped did not perceive of themselves as victims." Gilbert concludes that studies like Russell's and Koss's inflate rape statistics, encouraging the public to believe that sexual violence has reached epidemic proportions.

While researchers agree that the problem of rape must be seriously addressed, they disagree about the incidence of sexual violence. Commentators present debate on this difficult issue in the following chapter.

| "The problem of sexual assault has been magnified and the data misinterpreted, in part because the issue of sexual violence against women has become enmeshed in politics."

THE INCIDENCE OF RAPE HAS BEEN EXAGGERATED

Neil Gilbert

Many researchers have exaggerated the prevalence of rape, argues Neil Gilbert in the following viewpoint. Because these researchers fail to distinguish between rape and a bad but consensual sexual experience, he asserts, they have created the false perception of a rape epidemic, particularly on college campuses. Furthermore, Gilbert contends, campus antirape programs often perpetuate the stereotype of naive, defenseless women at the mercy of aggressive, forceful men. Such stereotypes demean both women and men and trivialize the problem of sexual violence against women, he concludes. Gilbert is Chernin Professor of Social Welfare at the University of California at Berkeley.

As you read, consider the following questions:

1. In Gilbert's opinion, why is Diana Russell's rape survey flawed?
2. What are some of the disparities between Mary Koss's study on campus rape and national rape statistics from other sources, according to the author?
3. According to Gilbert, in what ways do advocacy researchers use their studies to influence the public's understanding of heterosexual relations?

From Neil Gilbert, "Was It Rape?" *American Enterprise*, September/October 1994. Reprinted by permission of the *American Enterprise*, a Washington, D.C.-based magazine of politics, business, and culture.

At least one-quarter of young women will be sexually assaulted before they leave high school.

Twenty-seven percent of female college students have been victims of rape or attempted rape.

Almost half of all women will be victims of rape or attempted rape sometime in their lives.

These alarming statistics have informed many media reports about the prevalence of sexual assault against women in our society. By whatever measure, the problem is a serious one. But should we trust the statistics? A careful review of some of the research that has been done suggests that the problem of sexual assault has been magnified and the data misinterpreted, in part because the issue of sexual violence against women has become enmeshed in politics. . . .

BIASED VIEWS ABOUT SEXUAL BEHAVIOR

The most highly publicized figures on rape do not hold up under close examination. . . . For example, in her 1984 book *Sexual Exploitation,* . . . Diana Russell (professor emeritus of sociology at Mills College in Oakland, California) found that 44 percent of the women in her survey [930 women in the late 1970s] were victims of rape or attempted rape an average of twice in their lives. . . . Russell's estimates were derived from responses to 38 questions, of which only one of these questions asked respondents whether they had been a victim of rape or attempted rape any time in their lives. And to this question, only 22 percent of the sample, or one-half of women defined as victims by Russell, answered in the affirmative.

A considerable proportion of the cases counted as rape and attempted rape in this study are based on the researchers' interpretation of experiences described by respondents. Thus, in assessing these interpretations, one might bear in mind Russell's perceptions about what constitutes rape. She says, "If one were to see sexual behavior as a continuum with rape at one end and sex liberated from sex-role stereotyping at the other, much for what passes for normal heterosexual intercourse would be seen as close to rape."

RAPE ON CAMPUS

Quoted in newspapers and journals, on television, and during the 1990 and 1993 Senate hearings on the Violence Against Women Act, the Ms. Magazine Campus Project on Sexual Assault directed by Mary Koss is the most widely cited study of rape on college campuses.

Based on a survey of 6,159 students at 32 colleges, the Ms. study reported that 15 percent of female college students have been victims of rape and 12 percent of attempted rape, an average of two times between the ages of 14 and 21. The vast majority of offenders were acquaintances, often dates. Using questions that Koss claimed represented a strict legal description of the crime, she also calculated that during a 12-month period 6.6 percent of college women were victims of rape and 10 percent attempted rape with more than one-half of all these victims assaulted twice. If the victimization reported in the Ms. study continued at this annual rate over four years, one would expect well over half of all college women to suffer an incident of rape or attempted rape during that period, and more than one-quarter of them to be victimized twice.

The Ms. project was funded by the National Institute of Mental Health and its findings published in several professional journals, which is some indication of the clout the project has. Nevertheless, there are compelling reasons to question the magnitude of rape and attempted rape conveyed by this study. To begin with, there is a notable discrepancy between Koss's definition of rape and the way most of the women she labeled as victims interpreted their experiences: almost three-quarters of the students whom Koss categorized as victims of rape did not think that they had been raped. Moreover, in support of the students' own account of their experiences, 42 percent of those identified as victims had sex again with the man whom Koss (but not the students) claimed had raped them; of those whom Koss categorized as victims of attempted rape, 35 percent later had sex with their purported offender.

Inconsistent Data

As Koss reported in Judiciary Committee hearings in 1990, "Among college women who had an experience that met legal requirements for rape, only a quarter labeled their experience as rape. Another quarter thought their experience was some kind of crime, but not rape. The remaining half did not think their experience qualified as any type of crime."

A somewhat different account of how these same students labeled their experience was reported in 1988 by Koss and others:

a. 11 percent of the students said they "don't feel victimized,"
b. 49 percent labeled the experience "miscommunication,"
c. 14 percent labeled it, "crime, but not rape," and
d. 27 percent said it was "rape."

The fact that 42 percent of students classified as victims by Koss had sex again with the men who supposedly raped them was not mentioned in her testimony before the Judiciary Committee. In 1988 she originally reported: "Surprisingly, 42 percent of the women indicated that they had sex again with the offender on a later occasion, but it is not known if this was forced or voluntary; most relationships (87 percent) did eventually break up subsequent to the victimization."

"YOU HAVE THE RIGHT TO AN ATTORNEY. . . . YOU HAVE THE RIGHT TO REMAIN SILENT. . . . ANY PROPOSITION YOU MAKE CAN AND WILL BE USED AGAINST YOU IN A CASE ABOUT *DATE RAPE* . . . !"

Bob Gorrell/*Richmond Times-Dispatch*. Reprinted by permission.

But in response to questions raised elsewhere, Koss again offered different accounts of her data. In 1991, in a letter to the *Wall Street Journal*, Koss was no longer surprised by this finding and claimed to know that when the students had sex again with the offenders they were raped a second time and that the relationship broke up not "eventually" (as do most college relationships), but immediately after the second rape. In this revised version of her findings Koss explained: "Many victims reacted to the first rape with self-blame and thought that if they tried harder to be clear they could influence the man's behavior. Only after the second rape did they realize the problem was the man, not themselves. Afterwards, 87 percent of the women ended the relationship with the man who raped them." Koss went on to suggest that these students did not know they were raped because many of them were sexually inexperienced and "lacked familiarity with what consensual intercourse should be like."

These explanations are highly speculative. They also demean the judgment, functioning, and self-possession of young women. It is hard to imagine that so many college women, even if sexually inexperienced, were unable to judge if their sexual encounters were consensual. As for the victims blaming themselves and believing they might influence the man's behavior if they tried harder the second time, Koss offers no data from her survey to substantiate this reasoning. Although research indicates there is a tendency for victims of rape to blame themselves, there is no evidence that this induces them to have sex again with their assailant. There are cases of battered wives who stay on with their husbands under insufferable circumstances. But it is not apparent that the battered wife syndrome applies to a large proportion of female college students.

VAGUE SURVEY QUESTIONS

One part of the problem in the definition of rape used in the Ms. study is the vagueness of a couple of the questions in the survey. Although the exact legal definition of rape varies by state, most definitions involve sexual penetration accomplished against a person's will by means of physical force, threat of bodily harm, or when the victim is incapable of giving consent; the latter condition usually includes cases in which the victim is mentally ill, developmentally disabled, or intentionally incapacitated through the administration of intoxicating or anesthetic substances. Rape and attempted rape were operationally defined in the Ms. study by five questions, three of which referred to the threat or use of "some degree of physical force." But the other two questions asked were, "Have you had a man attempt sexual intercourse (get on top of you, attempt to insert his penis) when you didn't want to by giving you alcohol or drugs?" and "Have you had sexual intercourse when you didn't want to because a man gave you alcohol or drugs?" But what does it mean to have sex when you don't want to "because" a man gives you alcohol or drugs? How does one attempt intercourse "by" giving alcohol or drugs? Positive responses to these survey questions do not indicate whether duress, intoxication, force, or the threat of force was present; whether the woman's judgment or control was substantially impaired; or whether the man purposefully got the woman drunk in order to prevent her from resisting his sexual advances. They could conceivably mean that a woman was trading sex for drugs or that a few drinks lowered the respondent's inhibitions and she consented to an act she later regretted. While the items could have been clearly worded to denote the legal standard of "intentional incapacitation of the victim," as the questions stand there is no way to detect whether an affirmative response corresponds to the legal definition of rape. In 1993, Koss acknowledged that the drug and alcohol questions were ambiguous. When these questions are removed, according to Koss's revised estimates, the prevalence rate of rape and attempted rape declines by one-third.

IGNORING DISCREPANCIES

One of the reasons the Ms. study has gained so much credibility is that Koss claims her findings are corroborated by many other studies. This creates the appearance that the Ms. findings are independently verified by a cumulative block of scientific evidence. However, an examination of these other studies reveals the highly variable methodology and questionable definitions employed in them, along with the tremendous discrepancies among the findings. Koss and Sarah Cook (a doctoral candidate in community psychology at the University of Virginia) refer to one such study this way: "In a just released telephone survey of more than 4,000 women in a nationally representative sample, the rate of rape was reported to be 14 percent, although this rate excluded rapes of women unable to consent." This, of course, is close to the 15 percent rate of rape claimed by the Ms. study. What Koss fails to tell the reader, however, is that approximately 40 percent of the rapes reported in this study affected women between the ages of 14 and 24, resulting in about a 5 percent rape prevalence estimate for that age group. According to the Ms. study, 15 percent of college women are victims of rape between the ages of 14 to 21. Thus, for almost the same age group, the Ms. study found a rate of rape three times higher than that detected by the National Victim Center survey. Only by sweeping the relevant details under the carpet of "supporting literature" can the results of studies such as these be construed as independently confirming the Ms. findings. . . .

The most startling disparity is between the Ms. study's finding on the annual incidence of rape and attempted rape and the number of these offenses actually reported to the authorities on college campuses. Using her survey questions, Koss found that 166 women in 1,000 were victims of rape and attempted rape in just one year on campuses across the country (each victimized an average of 1.5 times). In sharp contrast, the 1993 FBI figures show that in 1992 at about 500 major colleges and universities with an overall population of 5 million students, only 408 cases of rape and attempted rape were reported to the police, less than one incident of rape and attempted rape per campus. This number yields an annual rate of .16 in 1,000 for female students, which is 1,000 times smaller than Koss's finding. Although it is generally agreed that many rape victims do not report their ordeal, no one to my knowledge publicly claims that the problem is 1,000 times greater than the cases reported to the police—a rate at which almost every woman in the country would be raped at least once every year.

DEMONIZING MEN

By promoting their figures on rape and violence, researchers who are also advocates seek to raise public consciousness about this issue. Raising consciousness can sometimes be positive. But they also seek to alter public consciousness by molding perceptions of the basic nature of the problem and of what constitutes the common experience of heterosexual relations. Thus, because they distort the issue, the effects can be harmful.

If it is true that one-third of female children are sexually abused and almost half of all women will suffer an average of two incidents of rape or attempted rape at some time in their lives, one is ineluctably driven to conclude that most men are pedophiles or rapists. This view of men is repeatedly expressed by some prominent activists in the child sexual abuse prevention movement and the rape crisis movement. As Diana Russell puts it, "Efforts to explain rape as a psychopathological phenomenon are inappropriate. How could it be that all these rapes are being perpetrated by a tiny segment of the male population?" Her explanation of "the truth that must be faced is that this culture's notion of masculinity—particularly as it is applied to male sexuality—predisposes men to violence, to rape, to sexually harass, and to sexually abuse children." In a similar vein, Koss notes that her findings support the view that sexual violence against women "rests squarely in the middle of what our culture defines as 'normal' interaction between men and women." University of Michigan law professor Catharine MacKinnon offers a vivid rendition of the theme that rape is a social disease afflicting most men. Writing in the *New York Times*, she advises that when men charged with the crime of rape come to trial the court should ask, "Did this member of a group sexually trained to woman-hating aggression commit this particular act of woman-hating sexual aggression?"

Given such perspectives, the sexual politics of advocacy research on violence against women demonizes men and defines the common experience in heterosexual relations as inherently violent and menacing. This is the message that is being delivered on college campuses, and a frightening atmosphere is the result. As social critic Louis Menand observes: "The assumption that sexual relations among students at a progressive liberal-arts college should be thought of as per se fraught with the potential for violence is now taken for granted by about just everyone." A similar message is being delivered to students at a very early age by sexual abuse prevention programs in the schools. Many of these programs make a point of teaching kids as young as three that male family members, particularly fathers, uncles, and grandfathers may sexually abuse children.

ARE WOMEN HELPLESS VICTIMS?

At the same time that all men are portrayed as dangerous predators, the most widely cited research on sexual violence conveys a view of women as helpless victims. In studies that claim to uncover the highest rates of rape, female subjects typically do not realize they have been raped, return to have sex again with the perpetrator because of guilt and self-doubt, are considered substantially impaired by any amount of drinking, and are often psychologically coerced by men into having unwanted sex. Regarding the latter, author Katie Roiphe declares: "The idea that women can't withstand verbal or emotional pressure infantilizes them." Writer Cathy Young points out that if failure to object to unwanted sex can be attributed to verbal intimidation or deficient will power, so can explicit consent. "Inevitably," she notes, "on the outer limits, this patronizing line of thinking reaches the conclusion that in our oppressive society, there can be no consensual sex." Indeed, according to University of Southern California law professor Susan Estrich, "many feminists would argue that so long as women are powerless relative to men, viewing 'yes' as a sign of true consent is misguided." Estrich herself agrees that in sexual relations a woman's yes may often mean no.

TRIVIALIZING VIOLENCE

Besides attempting to portray normal sexual relations between men and women as inherently brutish by equating vicious and appalling acts with a single unwanted kiss or attempted petting, advocacy research on rape and child sexual abuse redefines these violations in ways that trivialize serious violence against women. . . .

It is difficult to criticize advocacy research without giving the impression that one cares less about the problems of victims than do those who magnify the size of problems such as rape and child abuse. Advocacy researchers who uncover a problem, measure it with reasonable accuracy, and bring it to public attention perform a valuable service by raising public consciousness. But the current trend in research on sexual violence against women is to inflate the problem and redefine it in line with the advocates' ideological preferences. The few impose their definition of social ills on the many. By creating sensational headlines, this type of advocacy research invites the formulation of social policies that are likely to be neither effective nor fair.

| "The reality is that danger exists, and women should be aware of the risks."

THE INCIDENCE OF RAPE HAS NOT BEEN EXAGGERATED

Paula Kamen

In the following viewpoint, Paula Kamen takes issue with commentators who claim that antirape activists have inflated rape statistics. These critics, she contends, often fail to consider important aspects of the rape studies they criticize and end up misrepresenting the results of those studies. Statistics on sexual violence actually underestimate the prevalence of rape on college campuses and in society, Kamen asserts. Therefore, she concludes, more serious-minded dialogue is needed to combat sexual violence in a way that promotes women's freedom, self-respect, and autonomy. Kamen is on the advisory board of the Women's Media Watch Project of Fairness and Accuracy in Reporting, a national media watchdog group. She is also the author of *Feminist Fatale: Voices from the "Twentysomething" Generation Explore the Future of the "Women's Movement."*

As you read, consider the following questions:

1. In Kamen's opinion, what was the problem with the 1970s sexual revolution?
2. In what ways are Katie Roiphe's attacks on Mary Koss's data unfounded, according to the author?
3. What is lacking in the media's coverage of acquaintance rape, according to Kamen?

From Paula Kamen, "Acquaintance Rape: Revolution and Reaction," in *"Bad Girls"/"Good Girls": Women, Sex, and Power in the Nineties*, edited by Nan Bauer Maglin and Donna Perry (New Brunswick: Rutgers University Press, 1996). Copyright ©1996 by Paula Kamen. Reprinted with permission of the author.

A ntirape activism is part of a broad, hardly recognized, slowly developing sexual revolution of this generation. While the sexual revolution of the 1970s was largely about women saying yes (to really prove themselves liberated), a new movement is empowering them to also say no, along with when, where, and how. As a result, women are more closely examining what turns them off—and also what turns them on. They are daring to study and even critique what happens to them in bed. Young women are not content with the rules of the old 1970s sexual revolution, which have collapsed under the weight of their own rigidity— and stupidity. That movement, which was liberating mostly for men, has saddled women with too much old patriarchal baggage, including a continuing double standard for women, which discourages communication and honesty from both sexes. Activists are striving for a new model and new freedoms that offer pleasure and freedom from absolute rules, as well as self-respect, autonomy, and responsibility. Their movement is parallel to others I have seen become increasingly visible on college campuses, including efforts to gain reproductive freedom, fight sexual harassment, and secure rights for gays and lesbians.

THE ANTIFEMINIST BACKLASH

Yet, in the past few years, I have also seen the antifeminist skeptics eclipse all others in the popular press and in slick upscale magazines. While feminists come in all ideological shapes and sizes, the most "wacky" ones have always made the best copy. Most magazine articles addressing acquaintance rape take the angle that date rape is mostly hype, and seriously question the extent and even the existence of the problem.

A variety of critics, from lofty newspaper columnists to the writers of Saturday Night Live, have taken easy aim at "feminist antisex hysteria" by making fun of the extreme Antioch College guidelines, first widely publicized in 1993. The sexual offense policy from this small Ohio liberal arts college has come to represent feminists' supposedly overpowering rhetorical invasion of the minds of college students. The eight-page policy states that students must give and get verbal consent before "each new level of physical and/or sexual contact/conduct." "Sexual contact" includes the touching of thighs, genitals, buttocks, the pubic region, or the breast/chest area. The policy spells out six categories of offenses: rape, sexual assault, sexual imposition, insistent and/or persistent sexual harassment, nondisclosure of sexually transmitted diseases (STDs), and nondisclosure of positive HIV status. Complaints against violators can be brought before the campus judicial board.

Many conservative critics, including seemingly unlikely allies such as Camille Paglia and George Will, employing every defense mechanism on a psychiatrist's diagnostic chart, reason that militant feminists have invented the problem of "acquaintance rape" and use this term at random to describe bad sex or an encounter that one regrets in the morning. Since the topic of date rape is no longer sexy because of its last few years of exposure in the press, this related topic—date-rape hysteria—has come in vogue. In 1993, "exposés" of date-rape hysteria appeared as cover stories in Newsweek (in an article about "sexual correctness"), New York magazine, and the New York Times Magazine. Christina Hoff Sommers reiterates many of these claims in Who Stole Feminism?, boosted by three right-wing foundations that provided grants of at least $164,000 between 1991 and 1993.

FAULTY ARGUMENTS

A major leader of the date-rape hysteria charge was twenty-five-year-old Katie Roiphe, author of The Morning After: Sex, Fear, and Feminism on Campus. She says such feminist discussion confuses young women into mislabeling a wide array of normal, often unpleasant, sexual experiences as rape. Her thesis is that the battle against date rape is a symptom of young women's general anxiety about sex. They allegedly displace their fear of sex onto a fear of rape. Roiphe reasons that since some cases are false, all claims of acquaintance rape are unfounded; if one is against rape, one must also be against sex. Those that speak out against rape are nothing but malleable dupes of feminists or hysterics, liars, or prudes.

A major gripe of Roiphe and others is that educators are putting an undue burden on men by advising them to obtain articulated mutual consent. "With their advice, their scenarios, their sample aggressive male, the message projects a clear comment on the nature of sexuality: women are often unwilling participants," Roiphe writes in her book. Indeed, rape educators do admit that women have been forced to have sex against their will by people they know. In contrast, Roiphe portrays an idealized, "post-feminist" reality that places men and women in a vacuum, untouched by social attitudes and pressures.

The greatest threat of Roiphe's distortions is that they push acquaintance rape back in the closet. Roiphe is characteristically narrow in her definition of what constitutes a "real" rape—incidents of violence that can never be confused with "bad sex." In her 1993 New York Times Magazine article, she gives as examples of rape brutal assaults by strangers, such as those of Bosnian girls and "a suburban teen-ager raped and beaten while walking home from a shopping mall." To back up her argument, Roiphe takes liberties with data. Her "findings" that discredit date-rape prevention work are often based on out-of-context, second-hand, false examples of radical feminist rhetoric and flimsy "evidence" that questions the validity of professionally scrutinized scientific studies.

A DISPUTE OVER STATISTICS

A central target of Roiphe and others is a major, influential 1985 survey by a University of Arizona Medical School professor, Mary Koss, sponsored by the Ms. Foundation and financed by the National Institute of Mental Health. One of the study's major findings was that 27.9 percent—or, as most often quoted, "one in four"—of the college women surveyed reported being the victim of a rape or attempted rape since the age of fourteen, with a majority having known the assailants.

Roiphe, Sommers, and other critics have condemned Koss's findings as invalid without ever contacting Koss to get her side of the story or further information. Roiphe repeats the most commonly waged criticism of Koss: "Seventy-three percent of the women categorized as rape victims did not initially define their experience as rape; it was Mary Koss, the psychologist conducting the study, who did." According to Roiphe, "Today's definition has stretched beyond bruises and knives, threats of death or violence to include emotional pressure and the influence of alcohol."

However, as all these critics failed to report, Koss makes clear that she used a standard legal definition of rape similar to that used in the majority of states. Also, contrary to Roiphe's allegations, Koss did not make emotional pressure a variable in her 15.8 percent completed rape statistic. She does ask questions about "sexual coercion," but she does not include this group in the 27.9 percent statistic of rape or attempted rape.

Koss explained to me that she included in her figures women who did not label their experiences as rape because of the prevailing public misconception that the law does not cover such cases of date rape. Also, at the time of the 1985 survey public awareness about the possibility that an attack between acquaintances was legally rape was much lower than it is today.

Koss points out in her writings that the majority of her respondents who reported experiences legally defined as rape still indicated, themselves, that they felt victimized; she did not project this onto them. According to the study, as all these critics fail to mention, of respondents who reported an incident of forced sex (whether or not they called it rape), 30 percent considered suicide afterward, 31 percent sought psychotherapy, and 82 percent said the experience had changed them.

Another major attack on Koss's data is the inclusion of her question, "Have you had sexual intercourse when you didn't want to because a man gave you alcohol or drugs?" Roiphe and Sommers exaggerate the importance of this in distorting her one-in-four statistic. Sommers actually goes on to conclude that "once you remove the positive responses to question eight, the finding that one in four college women is a victim of rape or attempted rape drops to one in nine." But, as Koss writes, without factoring in this question, the victims of rape or attempted rape actually fall from one in four to one in five. Sommers took this error out of later printings of her book but still added that when this question is removed and you "subtract from the survey's results all the women who did not believe they were raped, the incendiary 'One in Four' figure drops to between one in 22 and one in 33."

THE PREVALENCE OF ACQUAINTANCE RAPE

Acquaintance sexual assaults are by far the most common type of rape both on and off the campus; however, they are rarely reported to authorities. Date rape (the most common type on college campuses) and acquaintance rape are estimated to happen to one-fifth of college women, whereas one-quarter of college women will experience either attempted or completed forced sex. These sexual assaults happen most often during the woman's first year, although a victim may also experience further episodes later on. Sexual assaults often happen to victims in the first week of college, before they know the social "rules." At colleges where first-year students live on campus and then must move off campus during their sophomore year, however, the incidence increases when students no longer have the protection of the structured college living environment.

Carol Bohmer and Andrea Parrot, *Sexual Assault on Campus*, 1993.

Koss's one-in-four findings reflect those of almost every major, peer-reviewed national and campus study, even though Roiphe and Sommers completely dismiss the existence and validity of this vast body of research. One of the most comprehensive of these studies is a nationwide, federally funded 1992 survey by the National Victims Center. It reported that of the 2,008 respondents contacted randomly over the phone, 14 percent reported a completed rape during their life, excluding cases when they were passed out or otherwise unable to consent. This is comparable to Koss's 15.8 percent statistic of completed rapes.

THE ONE-IN-FOUR FIGURE IS CORRECT

But, the most convincing evidence of the accuracy of Koss's study comes from the most accurate and comprehensive sex survey in America: the National Health and Social Life Survey (NHSLS) conducted by the National Opinion Research Center. In 1994, it was released in two books, one for a popular and another for an academic audience. The NHSLS found that, since puberty, 22 percent of women were forced by a man to do something sexually, and 30 percent of them were forced by more than one man. And even these numbers underestimate the true level of sexual violence in our society, as the researchers point out: "Because forced sex is undoubtedly underreported in surveys because of the socially stigmatized nature of the event, we believe that our estimates are probably conservative 'lower-bound' estimates of forced sex within the population."

In more than three-quarters of the cases, the perpetrator was someone the woman knew well (22 percent), was in love with (46 percent), or married to (9 percent)—only 4 percent were attacked by a stranger. These forced sexual experiences had an impact on women's lives. Fifty-seven percent of the forced women (versus 42 percent of the rest) had emotional problems in the past year which interfered with sex, and 34 percent (versus 18 percent of those not forced) said sex in the past year was not pleasurable. Twenty percent (versus 12 percent of those not forced) generally said they were sometimes fairly unhappy or unhappy most of the time.

The NHSLS data strongly confirm Koss's findings. It found that 25 percent of women eighteen to twenty-four had been forced to do something sexually. The survey also revealed that most of these attacks probably occurred when women were relatively young, since women eighteen to twenty-four had virtually identical rates of forced sex—about 25 percent. The slightly lower number of responses from older women can probably be accounted for by a greater reluctance to admit to being forced sexually and by a smaller number of sex partners.

These criticisms of Koss are not original or new. Roiphe and Sommers largely got their critiques of Koss's one-in-four figure secondhand, from Neil Gilbert, University of California, Berkeley, social welfare professor. Though Gilbert has never published anything about rape in a scholarly, peer-reviewed journal, he has written other critiques of Koss's research for the right-wing press. Gilbert's widely cited 1991 *Public Interest* article contains grave inaccuracies regarding Koss's data—falsely charging that Koss included "emotional coercion" as part of the definition of rape, for example. In Gilbert's 1991 and 1993 *Wall Street Journal* commentaries, his stated goal is to defeat the Violence against Women Act, which deals mainly with street crime and domestic violence and was finally passed after years of debate in August 1994. A 1991 press release issued by the University of California, Berkeley, boasted that "partly as a result of Gilbert's research, Governor Deukmejian last year canceled all state funding for the school-based [child sex abuse] prevention programs."

Despite Gilbert's partisan, nonacademic attacks on Koss's rigorously documented, peer-reviewed research, it is often Gilbert who is considered a scholar in press accounts and Koss who is treated as an ideologue. Even the *Chronicle of Higher Education* used this spin in a 1992 headline on the debate: "A Berkeley Scholar Clashes with Feminists over Validity of Their Research on Date Rape."

SUPERFICIAL MEDIA COVERAGE

In exaggerating feminist "date-rape hysteria," reporters from the popular press have clearly taken the easiest and most superficial route in date-rape coverage. The media has failed to report routinely and in depth about acquaintance rape. Instead, the issue is covered in irregular waves when sensational cases come forth (for example, the William Kennedy Smith case) or sexy controversy strikes (Roiphe's "exposé" of statistics). The press has barely broken ground in discussing the complexities, root causes, and influences of the crime of acquaintance rape—along with all issues involving violence against women.

When discussing feminism, as the Sommers and Roiphe coverage shows, reporters flock to "cat fight" angles. They pit an extreme antifeminist against an unwavering profeminist, giving the impression to the public that feminists all think and act alike and perceive the issues as clear-cut. Reporters too often take "scientific" criticism of feminists at face value, neglecting to investigate the supposedly refuted data.

Also missing in today's rape coverage is news about important efforts to curb violence against women. The press hardly mentioned the Senate Judiciary Committee's May 1993 report about the failure of the criminal justice system to recognize and prosecute rape, along with the status and content of the Violence against Women Act. The media rarely investigates the criminal justice system's failure to recognize and prosecute acquaintance rapes. This covers the spectrum from police who label reports of rape among acquaintances as "unfounded" to jurors who dismiss a rape victim because she doesn't look "terrorized enough."

The press also needs to focus its lens beyond the comfortable and familiar middle-class university to the less beautifully and neatly landscaped outside world, populated by the vast majority of young women. Rape and activism do happen outside of college campuses. Gone unrecognized has been community feminist activism and education, which are often concentrated at rape crisis centers. (Indeed, the sensational reports of young nubile coeds from white and middle-class communities are more sexy to viewers and readers.)

THE NEED FOR DIALOGUE

However, the level of activism is still often most intense at four-year universities, enclaves that Roiphe, a Harvard graduate and Princeton graduate student, knows well. This is not because women there are brainwashed and trying to grab "very oppressed victim" status, as Roiphe describes; the reality is that they commonly have more time and opportunity to speak out on important issues. They are doing what others would—if given the resources. Instead of scorning the activists as privileged, as Roiphe does, I appreciate them for getting the message out the best way they can. Simply criticizing these feminists for causing the date-rape problem just pins all of the blame and all of the responsibility to stop rape on the same old group: women themselves.

But reporters are only part of the solution to more complex and effective dialogue about acquaintance rape. Those feminists and antifeminists debating these issues publicly have yet to discuss responsibly and realistically the subject of danger in sexual experiences. One side, starring Camille Paglia and Katie Roiphe, describes danger as a natural and unavoidable part of sexuality and says that women should just do the mature thing and accept it. And feminists, usually the only ones in our society who dare to discuss how women are indeed victimized and advocate for them, too often singularly focus in public debate on the risks of sexual behavior and neglect to focus on the women's movement's historic goal to attain women's sexual freedom and autonomy.

We need to hear more arguments that go a step further: the reality is that danger exists, and women should be aware of the risks. But young people also have the right to expect safety. Fighting against date rape can also mean fighting for women's pleasure and sexual agency.

> "Whatever capacity we have to be glad
> about our existence, to feel unique
> and special and loved . . . , is stolen
> when an adult turns a child into an
> object of sexual gratification."

CHILDHOOD SEXUAL ABUSE IS A SERIOUS PROBLEM

Laura M. Markowitz

Childhood sexual abuse is much more prevalent than previously imagined, argues Laura M. Markowitz in the following viewpoint. She contends that children who are molested or sexually abused by adults experience deep and long-term psychological damage. According to Markowitz, many of these children cope with the pain of sexual abuse by blocking out conscious memories of the events. These memories, Markowitz maintains, often remain suppressed for years until flashbacks and painful emotions in adulthood cause survivors to enter therapy for help in recalling their memories and healing from the abuse. Markowitz is a senior editor at *Family Therapy Networker*, a bimonthly periodical for mental health professionals.

As you read, consider the following questions:

1. According to Markowitz, what did Diana Russell discover in her 1977 study on incest?
2. What are some of the difficulties in defining sexual abuse, in the author's opinion?
3. How did the incest victim Lisa dissociate from her experiences while she was being abused, according to Markowitz?

Excerpted from Laura M. Markowitz, "Reclaiming the Light," *Family Therapy Networker*, May/June 1992. Reprinted by permission of the author.

When Washington, D.C., social worker Rosalyn Beroza went through her family therapy training in the late 1970s, the topic of incest was never discussed or even mentioned in her classes, in her supervision, at the conferences she attended or in any professional literature she read. She didn't dismiss the notion that children were sexually abused by their relatives; she simply didn't consider it at all. Not surprisingly, she never had a client bring up childhood sexual abuse in her first eight years of practice.

In 1985, 45-year-old Carol came to see her with a variety of what Beroza thought were extremely odd symptoms. A professor of philosophy at a large university, Carol would often show up late for lectures or miss them altogether because she had gone into a spontaneous trance and lost all track of time. In addition, she regularly had uncontrollable urges to cut herself, and more than once had succumbed. One of these episodes finally frightened her enough to bring her to therapy. For several months, the therapy focused on her anger toward her alcoholic father, who had abandoned the family when she was 17, on her depressed mother, who had committed suicide five years earlier, and on Carol's inability to form any lasting relationships.

Eventually, it became apparent to Beroza that something had been left out of Carol's account of her life, and she began to suspect that incest might be the missing piece. "My immediate reaction was to jerk away from the idea," says Beroza. "My stomach churned and I felt revulsion, and also fear that I wouldn't know what to do if I was right about this. It turned out that asking Carol about her abuse was the turning point in the therapy. That was how I 'discovered' incest."

THE PREVALENCE OF INCEST

Beroza soon noticed that everyone else in her peer supervision group was coming to similar realizations. In the months that followed, everywhere she looked—in the workshop flyers she got in the mail, on the programs of national conferences, in the mainstream therapy journals—the taboo subject of incest was suddenly coming out of the shadows. Outside the field, talk-show host Oprah Winfrey revealed she was an incest survivor while interviewing a guest on her own show. Soon the talk shows were regularly discussing incest, and the news media followed. Largely as a result of this coverage, many clinicians found incest survivors flocking to their offices. "In seven years, my private practice has gone from including one incest survivor to now having two-thirds of my cases involve childhood sexual abuse," says Beroza, whose experience is by no means unusual. Today, it is rare to find a clinician in general practice who isn't seeing these cases. . . .

Recognition of the prevalence of incest has transformed . . . some popular clinical formulations. . . . "We used to have tortured ideological explanations for conditions we couldn't really figure out, like borderlines, multiple personalities, anorectics and bulimics," says David Waters, a family therapy teacher at the University of Virginia Medical School. "I don't know how many articles I've read that confidently explained how girls with eating disorders were afraid to leave home, or had emotionally distant fathers and overinvolved mothers. Now we know that many of these cases involve sexual abuse.". . .

Do we really believe that more children are sexually abused than wear braces? Than take piano lessons? Than go to summer camp? Than play in Little League? It is hard to wrap your mind around the statistics so often cited—that one in three girls and one in seven boys are sexually molested as children.

In a landmark 1977 study that first challenged the earlier conventional wisdom about the incidence of incest, Mills College professor Diana Russell interviewed 930 women in San Francisco and found that 38 percent had been sexually abused before age 18, and 89 percent of those abused had been molested by a relative or friend of the family. Russell's finding was a bombshell. Many of her colleagues had a hard time believing these numbers and wondered if the subjects might not have imagined the abuse or simply lied to the researchers. Some wondered whether the staggering numbers being cited were inflated by a bias toward finding incest. "Russell's survey used intensive, probing interviews, which may well have led to overreporting of abuse," says journalist Richard Wexler, author of *Wounded Innocents: The Real Victims of the War Against Child Abuse*. But a later study of the reliability of subjects' memories of childhood sexual abuse by psychiatrist Judith Herman found that 74 percent of those memories could be independently confirmed, and another nine percent were indirectly supported.

DEFINING SEXUAL ABUSE

But what exactly do these studies about childhood sexual abuse measure? Just what is being defined as sexual abuse? There are those who claim that the very term "abuse," sexual or otherwise, has become such a buzzword in recent years that it has lost any clear meaning. Adult-survivor groups of dysfunctional families, alcoholics, incest, codependence and divorce have mushroomed, making victim-identified communities one of the biggest grass-roots movements in our country. With so many individuals claiming to have been "abused," the word becomes deadening, not simply because it has been overused, but because, in becoming fashionable, it has come to mean too many things.

At the same time, the word "incest" makes us jumpy. We were all raised in a culture that treats women, children, and, increasingly, men as sexual objects, and as one therapist admits, we all have our prurient fantasies. "Mothers are always talking about how common it is to be stimulated by their babies," says Chicago family therapist Mary Jo Barrett, who pioneered in the systemic treatment of incest, "and years ago I read that something like 50 percent of men have gotten erections around their kids." Parent-child relationships are intimate and emotional, and also sensual. Parents like the softness of their child's skin, or playing with the child's silky hair. And children love to be held and cuddled and stroked by a loving parent. But our society sends confusing messages about love, intimacy and sex, sometimes lumping them all together. If parents come from traumatic backgrounds, or were abused themselves as children, they may too readily sexualize the intimacy and closeness they experience with their children.

So when does a parent cross the line between inappropriate behavior and incestuous behavior? Some overtly sexual acts are clearly transgressions, like intercourse, fellatio, cunnilingus, mutual masturbation and kissing or fondling of a child's sexual parts. But is it sexual abuse if a father leaves the bathroom door open when he gets out of the shower? Is it abusive if a mother gives her 11-year-old son a bath? Most therapists who work in the sexual abuse field insist such questions can't be answered categorically; that, as with all behavior, the therapist needs to understand the context. "It depends on what's going on when the father shaves naked in front of the kids," says Barrett. "Is he leaving the door open precisely so the kids will watch? Is he getting turned on by it? Are the kids uncomfortable? Is he leaving the door open because he knows they are out there and can't help but see him naked? Context is everything. The same act by one person in one situation may not be abusive, while from another person in another situation it most certainly is."

A Terrible Betrayal

Part of the problem we run into when we try to talk about childhood sexual abuse is with our language: there is a poverty of words that can adequately convey the terrible betrayal that takes place when adults sexualize a relationship with a child. Although it sometimes involves overt coercion, as in a violent rape, child molestation can be any act that takes advantage of the child's vulnerability and trust for the adult's sexual gratification. From talking to survivors, it is clear that whatever the actual abuse they suffered, it is the use of the adult's power over the child to manipulate the situation, and to make the child feel guilty, ashamed, disgusting and degraded that does much of the damage. Every situation of adult-and-child sexual contact will be abusive by virtue of the fact that the adult has all the power and the child cannot really say no. "In 100 percent of cases I've seen, people who were sexually abused as children—even ones who learned to initiate the contact as a way of trying to control their abuse—say they fervently wish it had never happened," says therapist David Calof, editor of the newsletter *Treating Abuse Today*. Frequency or severity of the abuse need not be the issue. Ellen Bass and Laura Davis write, in *The Courage to Heal*, "Betrayal takes only a minute. A father can slip his fingers into his daughter's underpants in 30 seconds. After that, the world is not the same."

A CASE OF INCEST

Early one morning, when Lisa was five, she wandered into her parents' bedroom to see if they were awake. Her mother, a nurse, had already left for her new, early shift on the intensive care unit, but her father was still in bed After she climbed up beside him to say good morning, he picked her up, sat her on his chest and started to tickle her. Then he was tickling her too much and it started to hurt. "Stop it, Daddy," she said.

"I can't help myself," she remembers him saying. "You're too adorable." She tried to wriggle away but he held her firmly and said, "Give dad a good-morning kiss." She kissed his cheek but he said, "That isn't good enough. Kiss me here," and pointed to his mouth. She kissed him on the mouth and tried to squirm away—she didn't like this new game. "Again," he said, no longer in a playful voice, still holding her. She kissed him, and this time he opened his mouth and forced his tongue into hers and moved it around. She fought to get away. He laughed at her struggle and said, "That's how grownups kiss. Someday you will kiss boys like that. Someday you will do other things to those boys." He made her kiss him several more times, although by this time she was crying with frustration because he wouldn't stop. When he saw her tears he told her, "Because you are so delicious, daddy couldn't resist. But if you tell mommy, she will be very mad at you for making me do that," then let her go. She ran out of the room.

That night, when her mother told her to kiss her dad good-night, Lisa ran away and hid behind the sofa. Her mother scolded her, "That isn't nice, honey. Your dad loves you, now give him a kiss." While her mother watched, she kissed him on the cheek, but as he picked her up to take her to her room, he winked at her and whispered, "We'll practice the other kisses later, when it's just you and me." She felt dirty.

REPRESSING MEMORIES OF ABUSE

There are many people in the field of psychology who recognize that children repress traumatic experiences as part of a very sophisticated coping mechanism. John Briere, from the University of Southern California School of Medicine, conducted a study on 450 subjects who had reported forced sexual contact at age 16 or younger. 59.3% reported amnesia of the sexual abuse at some point before age 18.

Another study was done by Linda Meyer Williams from the University of New Hampshire Family Research Laboratory. She studied 100 women who had reported sexual abuse as children and teenagers to a hospital emergency room in the 1970s. There were interviewed again in 1990–91, and told it was part of a follow-up study researching the health and lives of women who received medical care at that hospital. Of the 100 women interviewed, over one-third were amnestic or failed to report their childhood sexual victimization during the extensive interviews conducted with them. The research strongly suggests that a large proportion of women do not recall childhood sexual abuse experiences because they repress traumatic memory.

Off Our Backs, February 1994.

A few days later she woke up in the middle of the night to feel his hands touching her chest and then moving down to touch her genitals She pretended to be asleep, and finally he left. The next night, she lay frozen in her bed waiting for him to come. When he didn't, she decided she must have made the whole thing up.

BLOCKING OUT THE ABUSE

A few weeks later, it happened again. This time she sat up and looked at him. He was only wearing his undershirt, and she looked curiously at his penis, which she had never seen before. He had a funny look in his eye, and she felt scared She started to call for her mother, but he quickly smothered her mouth with his hand and shoved her on her back. "If mommy finds out about this, she'll be angry with you, and she'll find out what a bad girl you are," he told her. Lisa was confused. Was she bad? "Be a good girl and do what daddy says and nothing will happen to you," he said, but still kept his hand over her mouth.

That was the beginning of seven years of almost nightly sexual abuse at the hands of her father. Lisa's response, so typical among children during episodes of sexual molestation, was to dissociate from the experience. While it was happening, she recalls, she would leave her body and go across the room to watch what was happening to herself through the eyes of her rag doll, Grace. "It felt safe because my father never noticed Grace. He would never think to put his fingers, penis and tongue into Grace, or choke her, or make her say nasty things like 'Fuck me, please,' or tell her she was evil and turning him on and making him do it," says Lisa, now a 30-year-old dentist. Dissociating allowed her to grow up seemingly happy. She blocked out any knowledge of the abuse during the day and coped with her nightly torture by sending her conscious self out of her body and "into" Grace.

Incest damages a human being on many levels, from undercutting the ability to trust others to destroying the sense of safety in the world. Like survivors of other traumas, incest survivors have many of the symptoms of post-traumatic stress— depression, anxieties and phobias, mood swings and compulsions. But the deepest damage of incest is done to the child's soul: whatever capacity we have to be glad about our existence, to feel unique and special and loved because we are who we are, is stolen when an adult turns a child into an object of sexual gratification. A 5-year-old is very small, very new to the world. If you tell her the tooth fairy comes and trades her a quarter for the tooth she lost, she believes you. If you tell him he can grow up to be whatever he wants, he believes you. And if you tell her she is irresistible and because of that she is making you have sex with her, she, tragically, believes you.

DEEP SHAME

To those of us who have not been sexually abused, it is hard to understand the depth of shame incest survivors experience. No matter that the adult was responsible for breaking the incest taboo, the survivor feels disgraced. Most abusers use some form of coercion to gain the victim's complicity, telling them they are to blame or threatening them with physical violence, saying they will hurt or abuse other family members if the child doesn't comply, or, most commonly, assuring their victims that no one will believe them if they tell. Because children are completely vulnerable to the adults whose protection they need, they find it vital to believe their abusers rather than blame them. "What are their choices?" asks Calof. "Either they can feel no pain and preserve the family's 'reality,' or they can feel pain and lose their parents. To the child's mind, no pain is better than pain, and a bad parent is better than no parent at all." No matter how much they intellectually understand that they were not to blame, deep down they believe they should have done something—told someone or acted differently to prevent the abuse from happening. "Whatever kind of pleasure they got out of being treated special, having a secret with the parent or even from the sexual encounter leaves them with a tremendous mark of self-loathing and shame," says David Treadway, a family therapist in private practice in Boston.

ABUSE MEMORIES RE-OPEN WOUNDS

Those incest survivors who dissociate during the abuse often block the events from their conscious minds for years, only to have them sometimes flood back into their memories with alarming suddenness. The survivors' experiences of flashbacks can leave them traumatized again, as the firm ground of what they have always believed to be true shifts violently and reveals a nightmare world. "I had told myself that I had a happy childhood," says Lisa. "My father and I had a close relationship even up to the day I had my first flashback of him raping me. I couldn't hold that information in my head. I blocked out the memories again, but the flashbacks happened over and over until I looked at what it was I was trying to stuff down. Then, when I saw what monstrous things had been done to me, I remembered desperately praying that I was going crazy—I would have rather been a psychotic than an incest survivor," she says.

"I remember sitting in a restaurant, having a conversation with an old friend of the family when I was quite suddenly overcome by inexplicable, paralyzing fear," says Joe, a 23-year-old paralegal who was sexually abused by both his parents from ages 3 to 11. "It was very physical—my heart pounded, breath came short and my teeth chattered uncontrollably. I had the strongest urge to flee, and managed to make it to the restroom, where I leaned my head against the cold, tiled wall and thought, 'What the hell is this?'"

More powerful than memory, a flashback is a reliving of sensations and emotions, sometimes in vivid detail. You are smelling his aftershave, hearing his voice and your own child voice, as if this were happening at this moment and, most terrible of all, you feel the anguish you felt back then. Mary McNamara, a 31-year-old musician and carpenter in Virginia, was 26 when she had her first flashback to an incident of childhood sexual abuse. "One day I was feeling not quite right and started to get a headache, so I turned the lights off, and just lay in bed for about 30 minutes," she says. "Then, without any warning, the most gut-wrenching memories took me back to my childhood, right to that terrifying moment." She felt herself as a 5-year-old, the cloth of the too-small T-shirt she had on, the sunlight that hurt her eyes because she had just come from a dark place, and her body flush with anger. She heard her 5-year-old self saying, "You had no right to do that!"

A palpable difference between incest survivors and other clients is that the pain and distress from incest is less accessible to cognitive interventions than with other physical abuses. "I can say to someone who had a physically abusive father, 'When your father threatened you or attacked you, you felt hurt, you felt angry, you felt sad,' and we can talk about those feelings," says David Waters. Someone who was sexually molested as a child, on the other hand, can't feel much except shock and horror for a long time after they regain their memories. Having successfully avoided those emotions for years, the survivor's work is to reconnect the affect with the knowledge of the event. . . .

HEALING INVOLVES GRIEF

Sexual abuse is a physical violation, and survivors typically have issues around physical touch, sexual intimacy and even the sight of their own bodies in the mirror. McNamara describes how her body seems to shut down when she feels threatened. "It's not something I can control, nor is it something I choose," she says. "It was a coping mechanism during the abuse, but I still don't always feel parts of my body, and if I drew a picture of myself, it would be only half a body, with no breasts. My breasts are trying to come back to life after once having been very badly beaten to a dark black bruise. I may never be able to feel sensation of any kind there without the psychic pain overshadowing it." Being touched by anyone can still trigger intense fear and anxiety, she says. "It can drive me crazy, or embarrass me, like when I go to the dentist and have to talk to this person who is about to touch me, about moving slowly, talking to me, understanding my fear. One root-canal specialist kept laughing, and asking if I was afraid of the pain. Pain! Pain? I would rather feel pain than an intimate caress. I would rather feel the blade of a knife separating my skin than someone reaching out to me."

Love is one of the hardest emotions for many incest survivors to tolerate. When another person offers love, it brings home to them all the nurturance they were deprived of as children. "I feel less threatened with someone who is mean than I do with someone who is kind," says McNamara. "When my therapist sometimes surprises me with kindness, I usually break down and cry at that moment when the heart opens up to accept the love." Ultimately, the healing work of incest survivors is grief work; the opportunity to be a child, with delight and curiosity and a firm foundation of support and guidance, can never be replaced, and incest survivors keenly feel this loss.

"A growing number of those [adults] who had come to believe they were sexually abused are now retracting their accusations."

CHILDHOOD SEXUAL ABUSE HAS BEEN EXAGGERATED

Claudette Wassil-Grimm

A number of psychotherapists believe that adults who have re-pressed memories of being abused as children can recover these memories through therapy. In the following viewpoint, Claudette Wassil-Grimm criticizes repressed-memory therapy, asserting that therapists who use this technique often unwittingly implant false memories of childhood incest and abuse in their patients. According to the author, the widespread use of this therapy has led to exaggerated claims of child sexual abuse. Wassil-Grimm is the author of *Diagnosis for Disaster: The Devastating Truth About False Memory Syndrome and Its Impact on Accusers and Families*, from which the following viewpoint is excerpted.

As you read, consider the following questions:

1. According to Wassil-Grimm, what symptoms do Ellen Bass and Laura Davis claim are the results of child sexual abuse?
2. How do patients come to believe that they have been the victims of severe sexual abuse, according to the author?
3. Why are many people afraid to criticize repressed-memory therapy, in Wassil-Grimm's opinion?

From *Diagnosis for Disaster: The Truth About False Memory Syndrome and Its Impact on Accusers and Family* by Claudette Wassil-Grimm. Copyright ©1995 by Claudette Wassil-Grimm, M.Ed. Published by The Overlook Press, Woodstock, N.Y.

There is a heated debate raging in the mental health field. Many therapists who specialize in sexual abuse issues are loath to question any accusation of sexual abuse. They have seen clients retrieve extremely painful memories of incest and feel certain that no one would want to believe anything that horrible unless it was true. At the same time, many other therapists question the zeal of the "sexual abuse recovery movement" and worry that recovered memories of abuse are the result of hypnotic suggestion and group pressure.

This controversy has polarized psychiatrists, psychologists, social workers, and psychotherapists into two strongly opposing camps and has made a thoughtful, rational interchange between the two groups nearly impossible. Therapists who support all claims of sexual abuse without question usually fear that the opposition may turn back the clocks until sexual abuse is a hidden shame again. For many therapists, the greatest concern is that children will again become silenced victims.

A DELICATE ISSUE

The treatment of children who claim they have been sexually abused is indeed a delicate issue; even when a child withdraws an accusation, the therapist may justifiably suspect that the child has been threatened by the perpetrator or other family members and told to recant. It is a brave child, indeed, who can follow through on a claim that may destroy her family. For this reason, many concerned therapists would rather err on the side of believing too readily than fail to support a child in such a vulnerable position.

However, more and more frequently adults are being encouraged to uncover "repressed" memories of sexual abuse. Because the trauma of sexual abuse can be a root of many psychological disorders, some therapists have concluded that most psychological disorders are evidence of sexual abuse. And if the client does not remember being abused, those therapists believe forgetting does not mean the abuse did not happen; it means that the memory is repressed. Sexual abuse recovery programs that specialize in helping adults retrieve repressed memories have sprung up all over the country. Though the majority of participants are women, a growing number of men are taking up this issue. Indeed, the ratio of men to women involved in the recovery movement is no different from the ratio of men to women who seek therapy for any reason. . . .

Women (and increasingly men) are flocking to recovery programs in their search for emotional peace, and many are uncovering childhood memories of incest. Though the scenes that play across these participants' minds are obviously very painful and vivid, skeptics question whether these are recollections of actual past events or merely "false memories"—a kind of nightmare daydreaming similar to what fiction writers do when trying to create a frightening story.

Each side of the repressed memory debate has been compiling data on the nature of memory to support its own view. Bystanders are hard put to sort out the truth in this battle of the certified experts. While many adults who have recovered repressed memories of sexual abuse are adamant about the truth of their discoveries, a growing number of those who had come to believe they were sexually abused are now retracting their accusations.

BAD THERAPY AND FALSE MEMORIES

We believe that there is now sufficient evidence—within the therapists' own accounts of their techniques—to show that a significant cadre of poorly trained, overzealous, or ideologically driven psychotherapists have pursued a series of pseudoscientific notions that have ultimately damaged the patients who have come to them for help. If our conclusion is correct, the epidemic of repressed memories "discovered" daily in therapy settings proves not that our society is exploding with the most vicious sort of child molesters and satanists, but rather that psychotherapists—if they are possessed with a predisposition to uncover memories of abuse—can unintentionally spark and then build false beliefs in a patient's mind.

Richard Ofshe and Ethan Watters, *Making Monsters*, 1994.

In 1983, Canadian journalist Elizabeth Godley accused her mother of sexually abusing her as a child. In 1987, she realized she had been mistaken. It has been more than ten years since Elizabeth first uncovered repressed memories of sexual abuse. In a 1993 article in the *San Francisco Examiner*, Elizabeth described how she now sees what happened to her in therapy:

It was on my second visit to the therapist that she shattered my composure with a single question.

"Elizabeth, do you think you might have been sexually abused by your mother?"

Suddenly, I was flooded with nausea. Alarm bells clanged in my brain. I felt light-headed and breathless. Perhaps this was the reason I'd been in and out of therapy for so many years?

The therapist, a psychologist, was struck by my reaction to her question. (Later, when I expressed skepticism, she reminded me of this, dismissing my doubts as "denial.") Convinced we were on to something, she asked me to remember as much as I could of this traumatic event.

In my apartment that evening (I was 38 and living alone), I began to "remember." I was four years old, my mother and I were in the woods near our house, she forced me to do certain things. . . .

My "memories" blazed with vivid detail. I recalled the texture of the moss at the foot of a cedar tree, the smell of the damp earth, the glossy leaves and tiny red berries on a nearby bush.

It would be four years—four years in which I had no contact with my mother, and almost none with my father—before I would come to know these memories were utterly false, that I had conjured up this scene from my imagination.

Elizabeth was not a dependent child when she made her accusation, nor was she dependent on her parents when she retracted it. She is one of many adult women who have, in recent years, experienced "false memory syndrome" firsthand. As more and more women wake up from the nightmare of imagined incest, professional organizations such as the American Psychological Association and the American Psychiatric Association are investigating the problem to try to curb this trend. Sexual abuse specialists are beginning to reexamine their methods and eliminate those techniques that spark imagination to create false memories.

A CONTROVERSIAL BOOK

What has led some therapists to adopt unorthodox methods that are potentially harmful to their clients? The Courage to Heal, first published in 1988 and the most popular book being recommended and used by adult survivors and their counselors, was written by Ellen Bass, a creative writing teacher, and Laura Davis, a participant in one of her workshops. Bass openly admits that she began holding workshops and training professionals even though she had had no formal education or training in psychology or counseling. With sympathetic ears and unusual sensitivity, Ms. Bass and Ms. Davis were able to collect many stories from adult survivors of sexual abuse. The book offers a great deal of comfort, affirmation, and useful advice. However, the authors' narrow exposure to mental health issues has caused them to see everything through the lens of sexual abuse.

Though most professional psychologists quickly recognize the many errors of logic in this "survivor's manual," some therapists have blindly accepted the unproven assumptions of the self-help literature. For example, the symptoms of adult survivors of sexual abuse offered by Bass and Davis are so broad and all-encompassing that even a mildly emotionally disturbed person (or an emotionally healthy person having a bad day) could answer yes to many of their self-analysis questions. This is particularly true of the list of coping mechanisms believed to be caused by forgotten incest, including such behaviors as being controlling, spacing out, being super-alert, using humor to get through hard times, being busy, making lists, escaping into books or television, compulsive eating, workaholism, and high achievement.

ILLOGICAL ASSUMPTIONS

Similarly, most of the "symptoms" the authors describe in their chapter entitled "Effects: Recognizing the Damage" are also common reactions to any stress or trauma. A Vietnam War veteran could answer yes to many of Bass's questions, and an adult child of a dysfunctional family, especially one who was physically abused, could answer yes to most. But just because most people who were sexually abused have these symptoms, it is not logical to assume that most people who have these symptoms were sexually abused. This would be as absurd as declaring they must all be Vietnam War veterans, even if they don't remember ever being in the war.

My last point brings us to the greatest fallacy of all in the book. On page 81 Bass states that

> If you don't remember your abuse, you are not alone. Many women don't have memories, and some never get memories. This doesn't mean they weren't abused. . . .

> One thirty-eight-year-old survivor described her relationship with her father as "emotionally incestuous." She has never had specific memories of any physical contact between them, and for a long time she was haunted by the fact that she couldn't come up with solid data. Over time, though, she's come to terms with her lack of memories.

The adult survivor takes up the story here to explain how she coped with having no memory of being sexually abused by her father despite the fact that she had many of the symptoms:

> I obsessed for about a year on trying to remember, and then I got tired of sitting around talking about what I couldn't remember. I thought, "All right, let's act as if . . ."

> So I'm going with the circumstantial evidence, and I'm working on healing myself. I go to these incest groups, and I tell people,

"I don't have any pictures," and then I go on and talk all about my father, and nobody ever says, "You don't belong here."

Herein lies the problem. If Bass had had some formal training in psychology, she and the therapists she has trained would begin to suspect that a client who has been trying to remember sexual abuse for more than a year and has failed just might have some other problem. She might have a mood disorder, a personality disorder, depression caused by perimenopause, or any number of other problems that could produce the same symptoms. Though much of what the client receives from the incest groups—support, acceptance, sense of belonging—could be helpful for any of the above disorders, an antidepressant or estrogen might prove much more helpful. However, the sufferer will never discover these alternatives as long as the group of people she depends on keeps telling her that her whole problem and cure lie in remembering her sexual abuse.

THE RECOVERY MOVEMENT

Not long ago, the nation was swept by the adult children of alcoholics (ACOA) movement. As the leaders of that movement began to publish information and hold workshops around the country, many adults who had not had alcoholic parents began to flock to the workshops, saying that they related very strongly to the symptoms and feelings of ACOAs, and they found the meetings to be very healing. Rather than insisting that the parents of these adults must have been closet drinkers and that these adults must now force themselves to remember the smell of liquor on their parents' breath in order to be healed, the leaders of the ACOA movement acknowledged that one could have the same symptoms from a different cause. Thus, they popularized the concept of the dysfunctional family and broadened the base of people who could benefit from their workshops and advice. Out of this grew the Recovery Movement—an initially healthy, self-searching, grass-roots network that helps teach many adults how to overcome childhood emotional handicaps. As the "recovery" philosophy is stretched to fit many subgroups (overeaters, shopaholics, and women who love too much, to mention a few), it sometimes becomes distorted.

The adult survivors of the Sexual Abuse Recovery Movement are one example of how recovery philosophy, taken to the extreme, can become a destructive force. The lure of the social acceptance of these groups is very strong—so strong that the unafflicted often look in longingly from the sidelines. And, in the Sexual Abuse Recovery Movement, if you want to be approved of and accepted, if you want to have access to the movement's support groups, you must at least act *as* if you were sexually abused, whether or not you have any memory of being sexually abused. You are asked to suspend your judgment and trust that the other group members know more about what has happened in your life than you do.

For my research I used a number of sources to solicit interviews with women who believed they had been sexually abused. My request for interviewees ran in *Moving Forward: A Newsjournal for Survivors of Sexual Child Abuse and Those Who Care for Them*; the *Family Violence and Sexual Assault* Bulletin; and the *Retractor* (a newsletter for women who have realized their sexual abuse accusations actually stemmed from "false memories").

A SCENARIO OF A FALSE DIAGNOSIS

Commonly, such a woman goes to a therapist following a period of depression or to seek relief from a problem such as bulimia. She may be recently divorced or under some other stress. For example, one client had lost her job, witnessed her two-year-old child get hit by a car, had a miscarriage, undergone major surgery, and watched the building next door to her home burn to the ground, all within a period of eight months, before going to a therapist for depression. What was this therapist's diagnosis? The client's depression was obviously due to repressed childhood sexual abuse. Whatever the presenting problem, a poorly trained therapist enamored with the *Sexual Abuse Recovery Movement* tells the client that she has symptoms of childhood sexual abuse and that she cannot get well until she has recovered her repressed memories. The client is exhorted to read self-help books on incest, attend incest survivors' groups, and maybe attend an intensive weekend-long group therapy session.

After much exposure to others' stories of sexual abuse, the client develops some vague images of being abused. She is soon convinced that it was her father who abused her. First she believes it was one incident, but after much pressure to "remember" more she concludes that she was abused from the time she was an infant until she was in high school—and she "repressed" every memory! At this point paranoid thinking begins to take hold. The client begins to suspect that other family members were involved. She comes to believe she was also abused by her brother and her grandfather. Then she remembers the faces of neighbors during the abuse and realizes she was the victim of satanic ritual abuse that involved all her childhood friends. When she reports that she had a flashback of killing a baby and drinking the blood, she can finally stop trying to "remember."

Now she can begin to recover.

But those who have been through this therapy and have recanted say that what they needed to recover from, at that point, was the therapy. This typical scenario illustrates many of the "red flags" of bad therapy: the fostering of dependence, paranoia, isolation, peer pressure, and boundary violations.

Lynn Price Gondolf, a retractor who sought help for an eating disorder, had always remembered that her uncle had molested her when she was a child. But her therapist kept insisting that she was repressing other memories of sexual abuse, until he had pressured her to fantasize that her father had abused her too. Lynn has since recanted these accusations against her father and in a 1992 television appearance explained,

> I told my doctor—I said, "These memories feel different than the memories I have with my uncle." And his reply was, "Well, that's because you haven't owned these, you haven't claimed these, you haven't processed these yet." So I believe that the therapists that do this—I know—they have all the answers to every question you're ever going to ask. . . . They believe, probably, in what they're doing.

THE FALSE MEMORY SYNDROME FOUNDATION

. . . Many adults were sexually abused as children, and most of them have never forgotten. However, the number of "adult survivors" who have "recovered" so-called "repressed" memories and have had their lives painfully sidetracked is on the rise. In March 1992 a group of families falsely accused of sexual abuse formed the False Memory Syndrome Foundation (FMSF). Since then, the foundation has received eighty to one hundred phone calls a day from families who are apparent victims of false accusations. Recently, the FMSF has begun to get more and more calls from retractors—adult children swept up in the adult survivors' movement who came to believe they had been sexually abused by a parent and who now realize that their "memories" were the result of group-induced hysteria or therapist-induced fantasy.

At first the psychological community ignored the FMSF, and critics claimed that the FMSF was nothing more than an advocacy group for perpetrators of childhood sexual abuse. However, a look at the credentials of professionals who support the FMSF and serve on its board gives the organization a credibility that is hard to dismiss. Serving on the FMSF advisory board are more than forty professionals, both men and women (many of whom have doctorates in psychology and teach at prestigious universities such as UCLA, Stanford, Harvard, and Johns Hopkins), as well as numerous teaching psychiatrists.

Richard Ofshe, Professor of Sociology at the University of California, Berkeley, and board member of the FMSF, comments, "The recovered memory movement is a dangerous experiment in conformity and influence masquerading as psychotherapy. It's rapidly evolving into one of the most intriguing quackeries of this century."

Understandably, many mainstream psychologists who approach each client with an open mind and who have knowledge of the various psychological problems that could be causing the client's symptoms are growing disturbed by the popularity of the sexual abuse recovery movement and its one-cure-fits-all philosophy. Yet many have been reluctant to publicly criticize the movement's methods or therapists because accepting the conclusion that someone has been sexually abused, no matter what evidence there is to the contrary, is the more "politically correct" position. Opposing the recovery movement will target them as being part of the "massive denial and justification movement started by perpetrators of child sexual abuse" as one Provo, Utah, therapist described the FMSF.

However, the denial really seems to be on the part of poorly trained therapists with one-track minds who cannot accept that many psychological problems are caused by life-transition difficulties, trauma, or many other conditions besides childhood sexual abuse. Some therapists are biased by personal experience with sexual abuse, which makes them loath to question any suspicion or accusation, while others have schooling that is too narrow and is based on unprofessional self-help books rather than scientific study. In some cases, therapists have become convinced there is a national conspiracy of satanists perpetrating not only sexual abuse, but also bloody tortures, though neither the Federal Bureau of Investigation nor local police departments have been able to find any evidence to support this belief. For clients who mistakenly stumble into these therapists' offices (and for the families of these clients), therapy can become a nightmare that goes on for years, delaying treatment of the clients' real problems and costing a great deal of money and sometimes much more.

PERIODICAL BIBLIOGRAPHY

The following articles have been selected to supplement the diverse views presented in this chapter. Addresses are provided for periodicals not indexed in the *Readers' Guide to Periodical Literature*, the *Alternative Press Index*, the *Social Sciences Index*, or the *Index to Legal Periodicals and Books*.

Margaret D. Bonilla	"Cultural Assault: What Feminists Are Doing to Rape Ought to Be a Crime," *Policy Review*, Fall 1993.
Julie Brienza	"Sex Abuse, Criminality Focus of Justice Study," *Trial*, October 1995.
David R. Carlin	"Date Rape Fallacies: Can There Be Purely Voluntary Acts?" *Commonweal*, February 26, 1994.
Howard Chua-Eoan	"After the Fall," *Time*, May 9, 1994.
James Cronin	"False Memory," *Z Magazine*, April 1994.
Barbara Crossette	"Female Genital Mutilation by Immigrants Is Becoming Cause for Concern in the U.S.," *New York Times*, December 10, 1995.
M. Esselman and E. Velez	"Silent Screams," *People Weekly*, June 20, 1994.
Edward Felsenthal	"The Risk of Lawsuits Disheartens Colleges Fighting Date Rape," *Wall Street Journal*, April 12, 1994.
Elizabeth Loftus	"Remembering Dangerously," *Skeptical Inquirer*, March/April 1995.
Wendy McElroy	"The Unfair Sex?" *National Review*, May 1, 1995.
Ms.	Special section on domestic violence, September/October 1994.
Anna Quindlen	"Victim and Valkyrie," *New York Times*, March 16, 1994.
Elayne Rapping	"What Evil Lurks in the Hearts of Men?" *Progressive*, November 1994.
Stephen C. Rubino	"Suffer the Parents: Clergy Sexual Abuse of Children," *Trial*, February 1996.
Donna Shalala	"Domestic Terrorism," *Vital Speeches of the Day*, May 15, 1994.
Alice Vachss	"All Rape Is 'Real' Rape," *New York Times*, August 11, 1993.
Alice Walker	"A Legacy of Betrayal," *Ms.*, November/December 1993.

CHAPTER 3

HOW SHOULD SOCIETY ADDRESS SEXUAL VICTIMIZATION?

CHAPTER PREFACE

On a summer morning in 1990, Dartmouth College professor Susan Brison was walking in the French countryside when she was grabbed from behind, brutally beaten, and sexually assaulted. Long after this attack, Brison continued to experience symptoms of post-traumatic stress disorder commonly exhibited by survivors of disasters: extreme anxiety, depression, sleep disorders, and flashbacks of the event. Brison maintains that she found it difficult to live with these symptoms and to heal emotionally from the assault: "Even when I managed to find the words—and the strength—to describe my ordeal, it was hard for others to hear about it. They would have preferred me to 'buck up'. . . . But it's essential to talk about [the trauma], again and again." Eventually, Brison joined a rape survivors' support group that assisted her through the latter stages of recovery.

Support groups like the one Brison joined are an outgrowth of the recovery movement, a network of self-help programs made popular by the success of Alcoholics Anonymous. These support groups offer assistance not only for those recovering from various addictions but also for those suffering from the effects of abusive relationships, childhood sexual abuse, and other kinds of sexual trauma. Advocates of the recovery movement contend that these groups aid the healing process by allowing survivors to talk about their experiences in a supportive, non-threatening environment.

However, many commentators argue that these support groups are counterproductive because they encourage people, particularly women, to see themselves as victims. Women who claim to be victims of sexual violence often perpetuate the damaging stereotype of females as weak, vulnerable, and helpless, these commentators contend. In addition, some critics maintain that many people seek status as victims of sexual violence to gain attention and sympathy or to further certain political causes. For example, David Sykes, author of *A Nation of Victims*, contends that feminists often employ "shrill victimist indignation" when addressing the issue of sexual violence, trivializing and exploiting real pain and suffering for "political ends."

Whether support groups are an effective means of helping victims overcome the trauma of sexual violence is just one of the issues debated by the authors in the following chapter.

| "Proclaiming victimhood doesn't help project strength."

WOMEN SHOULD AVOID CLAIMING STATUS AS VICTIMS

Katie Roiphe

In the following viewpoint, Katie Roiphe argues that antirape demonstrations—such as the annual "Take Back the Night" marches held on many college campuses—encourage women to view themselves as actual or potential victims of sexual violence. Roiphe maintains that by speaking publicly about their victimization and their feelings of helplessness, activists at these demonstrations reinforce the stereotype that women are weak and vulnerable. Promoting this negative stereotype is not a constructive way to deal with the problem of sexual violence, she concludes. Roiphe is the author of *The Morning After: Sex, Fear, and Feminism on Campus*, from which this viewpoint is excerpted.

As you read, consider the following questions:

1. According to Roiphe, how are the speakers' stories at the "Take Back the Night" marches similar?
2. How does John Irving's *The World According to Garp* illustrate some feminists' obsession with "being silenced," in Roiphe's opinion?
3. According to the author, why did Mindy, the "Take Back the Night" march participant, falsely accuse a male student of rape?

It's April—leaves sprouting, flowers, mad crushes, flirtations, Chaucer's pilgrims, bare legs, long days, and marches against rape. Renewal means more than those practically obscene magnolia trees again, branches laden with Georgia O'Keeffe blossoms. Renewal means more than passing exams and drinking wine outside. It means more than enjoying the lengthening day: it means taking back the night.

A MARCH AGAINST SEXUAL VIOLENCE

It's a Saturday night. It's the end of the month and it still hasn't gotten warm. Instead of listening to bands, or watching movies, or drinking beer, more than four hundred Princeton students are "taking back the night." That is, they are marching, as one of the organizers says into the microphone, "to end sexual violence against women." In past years the numbers have climbed to a thousand participants. Carrying candles, the students march through campus, past the library, and down Prospect Street, past the eating clubs, the social hub of Princeton's undergraduates.

The marchers chant "Princeton unite, take back the night, Princeton unite, take back the night," and a drumbeat adds drama, noise, and substance to their voices. As they pass the eating clubs the chants get louder, more forceful. "No matter what we wear, no matter where we go, yes means yes and no means no!" It's already dark. They scheduled the march earlier this year, because last year's march went until three in the morning. "Hey ho! Hey ho! Sexism has got to go." As they march, girls put their arms around each other. Some of the march organizers wear armbands. This is to identify them in case anyone falls apart and needs to talk.

The ritual is this: at various points in the march everyone stops and gathers around the microphone. Then the "survivors" and occasionally the friends of "survivors" get up to "speak out." One by one they take their place at the microphone, and one by one they tell their story. The stories are intimate accounts of sexual violence, ranging from being afraid on the subway to having been the victim of gang rape and incest.

The marchers stand in Prospect Garden, a flower garden behind the faculty club. A short, plump girl who looks like she is barely out of high school cups her hands around the microphone. Her face is pink from the cold. She begins to describe a party at one of the eating clubs. Her words are slow, loud, deliberate. That night, she had more beers than she could remember, and she was too drunk to know what was going on. A boy she knew was flirting with her, he asked her to go back to his room—it all happened so fast. Her friends told her not to. They told her she was too drunk to make decisions. She went anyway, and he raped her. Later, she says, his roommates thought he was cool for "hooking up." She left her favorite blue jean jacket in his room. She finally went and got it back, but she never wore it again. She pauses. Later the boy apologized to her, so, she says angrily, he must have known it was rape. She stops talking and looks into the crowd. Everyone applauds to show their support.

As the applause dies down, another girl stands up, her face shiny with tears, and brushes the blond hair out of her eyes. I wasn't going to speak out, she explains, because I wasn't a survivor of rape, but I too was silenced. A friend, she continues, someone I used to have a crush on, betrayed my trust. We were lying next to each other and he touched my body. She pauses, swallowing the tears rising in her throat, then goes on: I didn't say anything, I was too embarrassed to say or do anything. I just pretended I was asleep. Distraught, confused, she talks in circles for a while, not sure where her story is leading her, and finally walks away from the microphone.

The next girl to speak out wears a leather jacket and black jeans. People think of me as a bitch, she says, her voice loud, confident, angry, they think of me as a slut. They think I treat men badly. But she explains that underneath her bitchiness is a gang rape that happened when she was sixteen. So if you see someone who acts like me, you shouldn't judge them or hate them, she says. Considering what happened to me I am in good shape, she says, I'm doing really well. It's just fucking great that I can even have orgasms. As she leaves the microphone, her friends put their arms around her. . . .

A SIMILARITY AMONG VICTIMS' STORIES

The strange thing is that as these different girls—tall and short, fat and thin, nervous and confident—get up to give intensely personal accounts, all of their stories begin to sound the same. Listening to a string of them, I hear patterns begin to emerge. The same phrases float through different voices. Almost all of them begin "I wasn't planning to speak out tonight but . . . ," even the ones who had spoken in previous years. They talk about feeling helpless, and feeling guilty. Some talk about hating their bodies. The echoes continue: "I didn't admit it or talk about it." "I was silenced." "I was powerless over my own body."

The catchwords travel across campuses, and across the boundaries between the spoken and written word. In a piece in the most radical of Harvard's feminist magazines, the *Rag*, one student asks, "Why should I have to pay with silence for a crime committed against my body? . . . I want you to know how it feels to be denied your own voice." Voicelessness is a common motif in Take Back the Night speak-outs. In 1988 the *Daily Princetonian* quoted one speaker as saying, "Victims shouldn't be silenced." At Berkeley, students organized a group designed to combat sexual assault called Coalition to Break the Silence. In the *Nassau Weekly*, Jennifer Goode, a Princeton sophomore, writes that Take Back the Night "counteracts the enforced silence of everyday existence. . . . This Saturday night the silence will be broken."

THE POPULARITY OF "BEING SILENCED"

These Princeton women, future lawyers, newspaper reporters, investment bankers, are hardly the voiceless, by most people's definition. But silence is poetic. Being silenced is even more poetic. These days people vie for the position of being silenced, but being silenced is necessarily a construction of the articulate. Once you're talking about being voiceless, you're already talking. The first Take Back the Night march at Princeton was more than ten years ago, and every year they're breaking the silence all over again. The fashionable cloak of silence is more about style than content.

Built into the rhetoric about silence is the image of a malign force clamping its hands over the mouths of victims. This shadowy force takes on many names—patriarchy, men, society—but with such abstract quantities in the formula, it's hard to fathom the meaning behind the metaphor. It doesn't matter, though. Almost all of the victims continue to talk about their silence.

It is the presumption of silence that gives these women the right to speak, that elevates their words above the competitive noise of the university. Silence is the passkey to the empowering universe of the disempowered. Having been silenced on today's campus is the ultimate source of authority.

One of the most scathing condemnations of the longstanding feminist obsession with silence comes from John Irving. In *The World According to Garp*, Irving tells the story of Ellen James, a modern-day Philomela: she was raped at the age of eleven, and her tongue was cut out by the rapist. Much to Garp's dismay, a group of feminists springs up around her, cutting out their own tongue in a gesture of political solidarity. They communicate through notes: "I am an Ellen Jamesian." They hold meetings and take stands. They dedicate themselves to the cause. When Ellen James herself reappears in the novel as an adult, she confesses that she hates the Ellen Jamesians. Beneath his comic, excessive, grotesque image of this feminist clan, Irving makes a realistic point about the feminist preoccupation with silence. He takes the political reality of feminists' insistence on identification with victims one step further: his feminists are so eager to declare themselves silenced that they are actually willing to cut out their own tongue.

As I listen to the refrains, "I have been silent," "I was silenced," "I am finally breaking the silence," the speakers begin to blur together in my mind. It makes sense that rape victims experience some similar reactions, but what is strange is that they choose the same words. Somehow the individual power of each story is sapped by the collective mode of expression. The individual details fade, the stories blend together, sounding programmed and automatic. As I listen to them I am reminded of the scene in Madeleine L'Engle's children's book *A Wrinkle in Time* in which a row of identical children play outside of a row of identical houses, bouncing a row of identical balls.

The *Rag*'s account of a rape ends "Thanks [to] the rest of you for listening," and an account published in the *Daily Princetonian* ends "Thank you for listening." As the vocabulary shared across campuses reveals, there is an archetype, a model, for the victim's tale. Take Back the Night speak-outs follow conventions as strict as any sonnet sequence or villanelle. As intimate details are squeezed into formulaic standards, they seem to be wrought with an emotion more generic than heartfelt.

SELF-CONGRATULATION

One theme that runs through all the speak-outs is self-congratulation—I have survived and now I am to be congratulated. Rhapsodies of self-affirmation may be part of "the healing practice," but as speaker after speaker praises herself for inner strength, they begin to seem excessive. From this spot in American culture, beneath Blair Arch at a Take Back the Night march, the population seems more oversaturated with self-esteem than with cholesterol. One common formulation at Take Back the Night is: "I am a survivor and it's a miracle every time I get a good grade, it's a miracle when I have friends, it's a miracle when I have relationships. It's a miracle. And I thank God every day." In the account in the *Daily Princetonian*, the survivor closes by saying, "If you don't know how to react next time you see me, give me a hug and tell me that you think I'm very brave. Because I, like all the other victims who speak out at Take Back the Night, am very brave."

In the context of Take Back the Night, it is entirely acceptable to praise yourself for bravery, to praise yourself for recovery, and to praise yourself for getting out of bed every morning and eating breakfast. Each story chronicles yet another ascent toward self-esteem, yet another "revolution from within."

THE "POWER" OF VICTIMHOOD

In the world of feminist victim ideology, women are routinely portrayed as debased, deformed, and mutilated. By construing herself as a victim, the woman, in this scheme of things, seeks to attain power through depictions of her victimization. The presumption is that the victim speaks in a voice more reliable than that of any other. (And in this world, remember, there are only two kinds of people—female victims and male oppressors.) The voice of the victim gains not only privilege but hegemony— provided she remains a victim, incapable, helpless, demeaned.

Jean Bethke Elshtain, World & I, April 1993.

As survivors tell their stories, as people hold hands, as they march and chant, there is undoubtedly a cathartic release. There is a current of support between listeners and speakers. At Columbia in 1992, students waited on line for hours to tell their stories, and as they did the listeners would chant, "It's not your fault," "We believe you," "We love you," and "Tell your story." The energy runs through the applause and the tears, the candlelight and the drumbeats. This is the same energy that sells millions of self-help books every year. This is march as therapy. . . .

A FALSE ACCUSATION

To be a part of this blanket warmth . . . , students are willing to lie. My first year at Princeton, one student was caught fabricating a rape story. Mindy had spoken at Take Back the Night for each of her four years at Princeton, and she had printed her story in the Daily Princetonian. What's interesting is that her account didn't really stand out; she sounded like everyone else at the speak-out. Her story could have been the blueprint. Whatever else anyone can say about her, Mindy could really talk the talk.

Her story went like this: she left the eating clubs after one boy "started hitting on me in a way that made me feel particularly uncomfortable." He followed her home and "dragged" her back to his room. The entire campus, as she described it, was indifferent: "Although I screamed the entire time, no one called for help, no one even looked out the window to see if the person screaming was in danger." He "carried" her to his room "and, while he shouted the most degrading obscenities imaginable, raped me." He told her that "his father buys him cheap girls like me to use up and throw away." And then he banged her head against the metal bedpost until she was unconscious. She then explained that he was forced to leave campus for a year and now he was back. "Because I see this person every day," she claimed, "my rape remains a constant daily reality for me." Now, she said, she was on the road to recovery, and "there are some nights when I sleep soundly and there are even some mornings when I look in the mirror and I like what I see. I may be a victim, but now I am also a survivor."

Unlike most participants in the speak-outs, Mindy put her story in print. Once it spilled over from the feverish midnight outpouring of the march into black-and-white newsprint, the facts could be checked. The problem was that she claimed she had reported a rape, and she hadn't. She claimed an administrator had told her "to let bygones be bygones," and he hadn't. She told people that a certain male undergraduate was the rapist, and he complained to the administration.

POLITICAL FICTIONS

In May of her senior year, 1991, Mindy came clean. Responding to administrative pressure, she printed an apology for her false accusation in the Daily Princetonian. She wrote of the person she accused, "I have never met this individual or spoken to him . . . I urge students who are knowledgeable of this situation to cease blaming this person for my attack." Mindy seemed to explain her motivation for inventing the story as political: "I made my statements in the Daily Princetonian and at the Take Back the Night March in order to raise awareness for the plight of the campus rape victims." So these were fictions in the service of political truth.

Mindy also claimed that she was swept up in the heat of the moment. "In several personal conversations and especially at the Take Back the Night March, I have been overcome by emotion. As a result, I was not as coherent or accurate in my recounting of events as a situation as delicate as this demands." If Mindy's political zeal and emotional intensity blurred the truth of her story, one wonders how many other survivors experience a similar blurring.

The accusation is a serious one, and the boy Mindy accused was in a terrible position in the community until she set the record straight. Accusations of rape stick, and in the twisted justice of the grapevine no one is considered innocent until proven guilty. Some may say, as an editorial in the Daily Princetonian did, that Mindy's false accusation was "an isolated incident" and shouldn't affect anyone's attitude toward Take Back the Night. Others would go further and claim that the abstract truth in these accusations eclipses the literal falsehood. In a piece about William Kennedy Smith's date-rape trial, Catharine MacKinnon, a prominent feminist law professor, wrote that the truth of a given accusation should be weighed in the larger political balance: "Did this member of a group sexually trained to woman-hating aggression commit this particular act of woman-hating aggression?" That people like MacKinnon are willing to sacrifice individual certainty to politicized group psychology only encourages the Mindys of the world to make up stories. . . .

THE SPECTACLE OF MASS CONFESSION

The line between fact and fiction is a delicate one when it comes to survivor stories. In the heat of the moment, in the confessional rush of relating graphic details to a supportive crowd, the truth may be stretched, battered, or utterly abandoned. It's impossible to tell how many of these stories are authentic, faithful accounts of what actually happened. They all sound tinny, staged. Each "I am a survivor and I am here to take back the night" seems rehearsed. The context—microphone, hundreds of strangers, applause—puts what one survivor called "deepest darkest secrets" under a voyeuristic spotlight. As they listen to the stories, people cry and hold hands and put their arms around each other. The few moments before someone steps up to the microphone are thick with tension.

As students throw stories of suffering to the waiting crowds, the spiritual cleansing takes on darker undercurrents. The undercurrent is the competition for whose stories can be more Sadean, more incest-ridden, more violent, more like a paperback you can buy at a train station.

Under Blair Arch, a blind girl takes the microphone and says, I have been oppressed by everybody, straights and gays, Catholics, Jews and Protestants. Unless I am imagining it, a ripple of unease runs through the crowd. There is something obscene about this spectacle. This is theater, late-night drama. One earnest male Princeton junior tells me "it was better last year. More moving. There was more crying. Everyone was crying."

Some of these stories may be moving, may be heartfelt and true, but there is something about this context that numbs. Once, over a cup of coffee, a friend told me she had been raped by a stranger with a knife. I was startled. Small, neat, self-contained, she was not someone prone to bursts of self-revelation. She described it, the flash of the knife, the scramble, the exhaustion, the decision to keep her mind blank, the bruises and the police. After she had finished, she quickly resumed her competent, business-as-usual attitude, her toughness, but I could tell how hard it had been for her to tell me. I felt terrible for her. I felt like there was nothing I could say.

VICTIMHOOD IS NOT STRENGTH

But an individual conversation is worlds away from the spectacle of mass confession. I find the public demand—and it is a demand—for intimacy strange and unconvincing. Public confidences have a peculiarly aggressive quality. As Wendy Kaminer writes in her book about the recovery movement, "Never have so many known so much about people for whom they cared so little."

Besides the shady element of spectacle, the march itself is headed in the wrong direction. Take Back the Night works against its own political purpose. Although the march is intended to celebrate and bolster women's strength, it seems instead to celebrate their vulnerability. The marchers seem to accept, even embrace, the mantle of victim status. As the speakers describe every fear, every possible horror suffered at the hands of men, the image they project is one of helplessness and passivity. The march elaborates on just how vulnerable women are. Someone tells me that she wanted to say to the male speaker who said "This isn't . . . a good night to be a man" that it wasn't such a good night to be a woman either. *Drained, beleaguered, anxious,* and *vulnerable* are the words women use to describe how they feel as they walk away from the march. But there is a reason they come year after year. There is power to be drawn from declaring one's victimhood and oppression. There is strength in numbers, and unfortunately right now there is strength in being the most oppressed. Students scramble for that microphone, for a chance for a moment of authority. But I wonder if this kind of authority, the coat-tugging authority of the downtrodden, is really worth it.

Betty Friedan stirred up controversy with a bold critique of the rape-crisis movement. She attacked the political efficacy of this victimized and victimizing stance when she wrote, "Obsession with rape, even offering Band-Aids to its victims, is a kind of wallowing in that victim state, that impotent rage, that sterile polarization." *Impotent* and *sterile* are the right words. This is a dead-end gesture. Proclaiming victimhood doesn't help project strength.

|"If thousands of Americans say that they are in psychic pain, I would not be so quick to write them off as self-indulgent fools."

WOMEN SHOULD ADDRESS THEIR FEELINGS ABOUT BEING VICTIMS

Mary Gaitskill

Mary Gaitskill is the author of the novel *Two Girls, Fat and Thin*. In the following viewpoint, Gaitskill argues that it is important for women who have been raped or sexually violated to come to terms with their feelings about having been victimized. Although some women's experiences may not fit the classic definition of violent rape, she asserts, that does not make their emotional pain any less real. Rather than condemning women for expressing their feelings and claiming status as victims, Gaitskill maintains, society should work to reduce the threat of sexual violence against women.

As you read, consider the following questions:

1. In Gaitskill's opinion, why was she unable to stand up for herself at the age of sixteen?
2. Why are people prone to exaggeration when discussing traumatic experiences, according to the author?
3. In Gaitskill's opinion, why was her experience of being violently raped by a stranger "not especially traumatic"?

In the early 1970s, I had an experience that could be described as acquaintance rape. Actually, I have had two or three such experiences, but this one most dramatically fits the profile. I was sixteen and staying in the apartment of a slightly older girl I'd just met in a seedy community center in Detroit. I'd been in her apartment for a few days when an older guy she knew came over and asked us if we wanted to drop some acid. In those years, doing acid with complete strangers was consistent with my idea of a possible good time, so I said yes. When I started peaking, my hostess decided she had to go see her boyfriend, and there I was, alone with this guy, who, suddenly, was in my face.

A SEXUAL VIOLATION

He seemed to be coming on to me, but I wasn't sure. My perception was quite loopy, and on top of that he was black and urban-poor, which meant that I, being very inexperienced and suburban-white, did not know how to read him the way I might have read another white kid. I tried to distract him with conversation, but it was hard, considering that I was having trouble with logical sentences, let alone repartee. During one long silence, I asked him what he was thinking. Avoiding my eyes, he answered, "That if I wasn't such a nice guy you could really be getting screwed." The remark sounded to me like a threat, albeit a low-key one. But instead of asking him to explain himself or to leave, I changed the subject. Some moments later, when he put his hand on my leg, I let myself be drawn into sex because I could not face the idea that if I said no, things might get ugly. I don't think he had any idea how unwilling I was—the cultural unfamiliarity cut both ways—and I suppose he may have thought that all white girls just kind of lie there and don't do or say much. My bad time was made worse by his extreme gentleness; he was obviously trying very hard to please me, which, for reasons I didn't understand, broke my heart. Even as inexperienced as I was, I sensed that in his own way he intended a romantic encounter.

For some time afterward I described this event as "the time I was raped." I knew when I said it that the statement wasn't quite accurate, that I hadn't, after all, said no. Yet it felt accurate to me. In spite of my ambiguous, even empathic feelings for my unchosen partner, unwanted sex on acid is a nightmare, and I did feel violated by the experience. At times I even flat-out lied about what had happened, grossly exaggerating the violence and the threat—not out of shame or guilt, but because the pumped-up version was more congruent with my feelings of violation than the confusing facts. Every now and then, in the middle of telling an exaggerated version of the story, I would remember the actual man and internally pause, uncertain of how the memory squared with what I was saying or where my sense of violation was coming from—and then I would continue with my story. I am ashamed to admit this, both because it is embarrassing to me and because I am afraid the admission could be taken as evidence that women lie "to get revenge." I want to stress that I would not have lied that way in court or in any other context that might have had practical consequences; it didn't even occur to me to take my case to court. My lies were told not for revenge but in service of what I felt to be the metaphorical truth.

Truth Is Complicated

I remember my experience in Detroit, including its aftermath, every time I hear or read yet another discussion of what constitutes "date rape." I remember it when yet another critic castigates "victimism" and complains that everyone imagines himself or herself to be a victim and that no one accepts responsibility anymore. I could imagine telling my story as a verification that rape occurs by subtle threat as well as by overt force. I could also imagine telling it as if I were one of those crybabies who want to feel like victims. Both stories would be true and not true. The complete truth is more complicated than most of the intellectuals who have written scolding essays on victimism seem willing to accept. I didn't understand my own story fully until I described it to an older woman many years later, as a proof of the unreliability of feelings. "Oh, I think your feelings were reliable," she returned. "It sounds like you were raped. It sounds like you raped yourself." I immediately knew that what she said was true, that in failing even to try to speak up for myself, I had, in a sense, raped myself.

I don't say this in a tone of self-recrimination. I was in a difficult situation: I was very young, and he was aggressive. But my inability to speak for myself—to *stand up* for myself—had little to do with those facts. I was unable to stand up for myself because I had never been taught how.

Conflicting Rules

When I was growing up in the 1960s, I was taught by the adult world that good girls never had sex and bad girls did. This rule had clarity going for it but little else; as it was presented to me, it allowed no room for what I actually might feel, what I might want or not want. Within the confines of this rule, I didn't count for much, and I quite vigorously rejected it. Then came the less clear "rules" of cultural trend and peer example that said that if you were cool you wanted to have sex as much as possible with as many people as possible. This message was never stated as a rule, but, considering how absolutely it was woven into the social etiquette of the day (at least in the circles I cared about), it may as well have been. It suited me better than the adults' rule—it allowed me my sexuality, at least—but again it didn't take into account what I might actually want or not want.

The encounter in Detroit, however, had nothing to do with being good or bad, cool or uncool. It was about someone wanting something I didn't want. Since I had been taught only how to follow rules that were somehow more important than I was, I didn't know what to do in a situation where no rules obtained and that required me to speak up on my own behalf. I had never been taught that my behalf mattered. And so I felt helpless, even victimized, without really knowing why. . . .

Unspoken Assumptions About Victims

Recently I heard a panel of feminists on talk radio advocating that laws be passed prohibiting men from touching or making sexual comments to women on the street. Listeners called in to express reactions both pro and con, but the one I remember was a woman who said, "If a man touches me and I don't want it, I don't need a law. I'm gonna beat the hell out of him." The panelists were silent. Then one of them responded in an uncertain voice, "I guess I just never learned how to do that." I understood that the feminist might not want to get into a fistfight with a man likely to be a lot bigger than she, but if her self-respect was so easily shaken by an obscene comment made by some slob on the street, I wondered, how did she expect to get through life? She was exactly the kind of woman whom the cultural critics Camille Paglia and Katie Roiphe have derided as a "rape-crisis feminist"—puritans, sissies, closet-Victorian ladies who want to legislate the ambiguity out of sex. It was very easy for me to feel self-righteous, and I muttered sarcastically at my radio as the panel yammered about self-esteem.

I was conflicted, however. If there had been a time in my own life when I couldn't stand up for myself, how could I expect other people to do it? It could be argued that the grown women on the panel should be more capable than a sixteen-year-old girl whacked out on acid. But such a notion presupposes that people develop at a predictable rate or react to circumstances by coming to universally agreed-upon conclusions.

This is the crucial unspoken presumption at the center of the date-rape debate as well as of the larger discourse on victimism. It is a presumption that in a broad but potent sense reminds me of a rule.

VICTIMS' RESPONSES TO RAPE

It is important to emphasize that not all rape victims suffer to the same degree with regard to rape trauma syndrome. Some show such tremendous distress that their ability to get out of bed in the morning is severely taxed. Other rape victims may seem to hold up fairly well, showing relatively few symptoms. Exactly how a person will respond after being raped may depend on several factors, including demographic characteristics, her own unique personal history, the circumstances of the rape, and the availability of later social support.

Julie A. Allison and Lawrence S. Wrightsman, *Rape:The Misunderstood Crime*, 1993.

Feminists who postulate that boys must obtain a spelled-out "yes" before having sex are trying to establish rules, cut in stone, that will apply to any and every encounter and that every responsible person must obey. The new rule resembles the old good girl/bad girl rule not only because of its implicit suggestion that girls have to be protected but also because of its absolute nature, its iron-fisted denial of complexity and ambiguity. I bristle at such a rule and so do a lot of other people. But should we really be so puzzled and indignant that another rule has been presented? If people have been brought up believing that to be responsible is to obey certain rules, what are they going to do with a can of worms like "date rape" except try to make new rules that they see as more fair or useful than the old ones?

THE PRESUMPTIONS OF "RAPE-CRISIS" CRITICS

But the "rape-crisis feminists" are not the only absolutists here; their critics play the same game. Camille Paglia, author of *Sexual Personae*, has stated repeatedly that any girl who goes alone into a frat house and proceeds to tank up is cruising for a gang bang, and if she doesn't know that, well, then she's "an idiot." The remark is most striking not for its crude unkindness but for its reductive solipsism. It assumes that all college girls have had the same life experiences as Paglia, and have come to the same conclusions about them. By the time I got to college, I'd been living away from home for years and had been around the block several times. I never went to a frat house, but I got involved with men who lived in rowdy "boy houses" reeking of dirty socks and rock and roll. I would go over, drink, and spend the night with my lover of the moment; it never occurred to me that I was in danger of being gang-raped, and if I had been, I would have been shocked and badly hurt. My experience, though some of it had been bad, hadn't led me to conclude that boys plus alcohol equals gang bang, and I was not naive or idiotic. Katie Roiphe, author of *The Morning After: Fear, Sex, and Feminism on Campus*, criticizes girls who, in her view, create a myth of false innocence: "But did these twentieth-century girls, raised on Madonna videos and the six o'clock news, really trust that people were good until they themselves were raped? Maybe. Were these girls, raised on horror movies and glossy Hollywood sex scenes, really as innocent as all that?" I am sympathetic to Roiphe's annoyance, but I'm surprised that a smart chick like her apparently doesn't know that people process information and imagery (like Madonna videos and the news) with a complex subjectivity that doesn't in any predictable way alter their ideas about what they can expect from life.

Roiphe and Paglia are not exactly invoking rules, but their comments seem to derive from a belief that everyone except idiots interprets information and experience in the same way. In that sense, they are not so different in attitude from those ladies dedicated to establishing feminist-based rules and regulations for sex. Such rules, just like the old rules, assume a certain psychological uniformity of experience, a right way.

POLITICAL PLOYS OR EMOTIONAL TRUTHS?

The accusatory and sometimes painfully emotional rhetoric conceals an attempt not only to make new rules but also to codify experience. The "rape-crisis feminists" obviously speak for many women and girls who have been raped or have felt raped in a wide variety of circumstances. They would not get so much play if they were not addressing a widespread and real experience of violation and hurt. By asking, "Were they really so innocent?" Roiphe doubts the veracity of the experience she presumes to address because it doesn't square with hers or with that of her friends. Having not felt violated herself—even though she says she has had an experience that many would now call date rape—she cannot understand, or even quite believe, that anyone else would feel violated in similar circumstances. She therefore believes all the fuss to be a political ploy or, worse, a retrograde desire to return to crippling ideals of helpless femininity. In turn, Roiphe's detractors, who have not had her more sanguine "morning after" experience, believe her to be ignorant and callous, or a secret rape victim in deep denial. Both camps, believing their own experience to be the truth, seem unwilling to acknowledge the emotional truth on the other side.

It is at this point that the "date-rape debate" resembles the bigger debate about how and why Americans seem so eager to identify themselves and be identified by others as victims. Book after article has appeared, written in baffled yet hectoring language, deriding the P.C. (politically correct) goody-goodies who want to play victim and the spoiled, self-centered fools who attend twelve-step programs, meditate on their inner child, and study pious self-help books. The revisionist critics have all had a lot of fun with the recovery movement, getting into high dudgeon over those materially well-off people who describe their childhoods as "holocausts" and winding up with a fierce exhortation to return to rationality. Rarely do such critics make any but the most superficial attempt to understand why the population might behave thus.

EXAGGERATION IS AN ATTEMPT TO EXPLAIN

In a fussing, fuming 1991 essay that has almost become a prototype of the genre, David Rieff expressed his outrage and bewilderment that affluent people would feel hurt and disappointed by life. He angrily contrasted rich Americans obsessed with their inner children to Third World parents concerned with feeding their actual children. On the most obvious level, the contrast is one that needs to be made, but I question Rieff's idea that suffering is one definable thing, that he knows what it is, and that since certain kinds of emotional pain don't fit this definition they can't really exist. This idea doesn't allow him to have much respect for other people's experience—or even to see it. It may be ridiculous and perversely self-aggrandizing for most people to describe whatever was bad about their childhood as a "holocaust," but I suspect that when people talk like that they are saying that as children they were not given enough of what they would later need in order to know who they are or to live truly responsible lives. Thus they find themselves in a state of bewildering loss that they can't articulate, except by wild exaggeration—much like I defined my inexplicable feelings after my Detroit episode. "Holocaust" may be a grossly inappropriate exaggeration. But to speak in exaggerated metaphors about psychic injury is not so much the act of a crybaby as it is a distorted attempt to explain one's own experience. I think the distortion comes from a desperate desire to make one's experience have consequence in the eyes of others, and that such desperation comes from a crushing doubt that one's own experience counts at all.

In her book *I'm Dysfunctional, You're Dysfunctional*, Wendy Kaminer speaks harshly of women in some twelve-step programs who talk about being metaphorically raped. "It is an article of faith here that suffering is relative; no one says she'd rather be raped metaphorically than in fact," she writes, as if not even a crazy person would prefer a literal rape to a metaphorical one. But actually, I might. About two years after my "rape" in Detroit, I was raped for real. The experience was terrifying: my attacker repeatedly said he was going to kill me, and I thought he might. The terror was acute, but after it was over it actually affected me less than many other mundane instances of emotional brutality I've suffered or seen other people suffer. Frankly, I've been scarred more by experiences I had on the playground in elementary school. I realize that the observation may seem bizarre, but for me the rape was a clearly defined act, perpetrated upon me by a crazy asshole whom I didn't know or trust; it had nothing to do with me or who I was, and so, when it was over, it was relatively easy to dismiss. Emotional cruelty is more complicated. Its motives are often impossible to understand, and it is sometimes committed by people who say they like or even love you. Nearly always it's hard to know whether you played a role in what happened, and, if so, what the role was. The experience *sticks* to you. By the time I was raped I had seen enough emotional cruelty to feel that the rape, although bad, was not especially traumatic.

EMOTIONAL TRUTH DESERVES SCRUTINY

My response may seem strange to some, but my point is that pain can be an experience that defies codification. If thousands of Americans say that they are in psychic pain, I would not be so quick to write them off as self-indulgent fools. A metaphor like "the inner child" may be silly and schematic, but it has a fluid subjectivity, especially when projected out into the world by such a populist notion as "recovery." Ubiquitous recovery-movement phrases like "We're all victims" and "We're all co-dependent" may not seem to leave a lot of room for interpretation, but they are actually so vague that they beg for interpretation and projection. Such phrases may be fair game for ridicule, but it is shallow to judge them on their face value, as if they hold the same meaning for everyone. . . .

Many critics of the self-help culture argue against treating emotional or metaphoric reality as if it were equivalent to objective reality. I agree that they are not the same. But emotional truth is often bound up with truth of a more objective kind and must be taken into account. This is especially true of conundrums such as date rape and victimism, both of which often are discussed in terms of unspoken assumptions about emotional truth anyway. Sarah Crichton, in a cover story for Newsweek on "Sexual Correctness," described the "strange detour" taken by some feminists and suggested that "we're not creating a society of Angry Young Women. These are Scared Little Girls." The comment is both contemptuous and superficial; it shows no interest in why girls might be scared. By such logic, anger implicitly is deemed to be the more desirable emotional state because it appears more potent, and "scared" is used as a pejorative. It's possible to shame a person into hiding his or her fear, but if you don't address the cause of the fear, it won't go away. Crichton ends her piece by saying, "Those who are growing up in environments where they don't have to figure out what the rules should be, but need only follow what's been prescribed, are being robbed of the most important lesson there is to learn. And that's how to live." I couldn't agree more. But unless you've been taught how to think for yourself, you'll have a hard time figuring out your own rules, and you'll feel scared—especially when there is real danger of sexual assault.

"The problem [with abuse-survivor books] is not with the advice they offer to victims, but with their effort to create victims."

THE INCEST-SURVIVOR MOVEMENT IS COUNTERPRODUCTIVE

Carol Tavris

In the following viewpoint, Carol Tavris takes issue with popular self-help books that focus on childhood incest and the repression of memories of childhood abuse. According to Tavris, because the authors of these books claim that almost any emotional problem—as well as the inability to remember any abuse—is a symptom of past sexual abuse, many people have come to wrongly believe that they were sexually abused as children. Furthermore, she asserts, these books often encourage incest survivors to place all the blame for their current problems on past abuse. This personal focus on the past does nothing to change society's complacency about sexual abuse, Tavris concludes. Tavris, a social psychologist, is the author of *The Mismeasure of Woman*.

As you read, consider the following questions:

1. According to Tavris, what symptoms do incest-survivor self-help manuals list as indicators of past sexual abuse?
2. How does Jean Piaget's "kidnapping" illustrate the problem of relying on childhood memories, in the author's opinion?
3. According to Louise Armstrong, as cited by Tavris, how has public dialogue about incest changed since the late 1970s?

How often do you suffer from the following symptoms?
- You feel that you're bad, dirty or ashamed.
- You feel powerless, like a victim.
- You feel that there's something wrong with you deep down inside; that if people really knew you, they would leave.
- You feel unable to protect yourself in dangerous situations.
- You have no sense of your own interests, talents or goals.
- You have trouble feeling motivated.
- You feel you have to be perfect.

This checklist, from Ellen Bass and Laura Davis's book *The Courage to Heal*, is supposed to identify the symptoms of incest. The trouble is that the same list could be used to identify oneself as someone who loves too much, someone who suffers from self-defeating personality disorder, or a mere human being in the late 20th century. The list is general enough to include everybody at least sometimes. Nobody doesn't fit it.

The Courage to Heal is the bible of the incest-recovery movement. It was published in 1988 and according to its publisher, HarperCollins, has sold more than 500,000 copies. It begat *The Courage to Heal Workbook*, which begat the authors' *Allies in Healing*, as well as Wendy Maltz and Beverly Holman's *Incest and Sexuality*, Beverly Engel's *Right to Innocence* and E. Sue Blume's *Secret Survivors*. To read these handbooks is to learn that almost any problem you have may be an indicator of abuse. Ms. Blume offers a 34-item "incest survivors' aftereffects checklist" of symptoms, which range from fear of being alone in the dark to multiple personality disorder—with phobias, arthritis, low self-esteem, wearing baggy clothes, the desire to change one's name and sexual difficulties in between. For Ms. Engel, the checklist includes feeling ugly and worthless, having a tendency to apologize inappropriately, feeling like a failure, jeopardizing chances of success, feeling helpless, having problems with sex or in relationships.... Why, it's the all-purpose female checklist.

THE ABUSE-SURVIVOR MACHINE

To want to throw a small wrench into the abuse-survivor machine is like opposing censorship of pornography: nowadays, you feel you have to apologize for any support you might be providing to molesters, rapists, pedophiles and other misogynists. This need for throat-clearing is itself a problem, one that results from the terrible polarization that has emerged on the subject of the sexual abuse of children.

One side, primarily committed to protecting children emphasizes the appalling prevalence of the abuse of childr the tendency of adults, in every generation, to deny or diminish the reality of this abuse. The other side, primarily committed to protecting adults, is concerned that in the contemporary hysteria too many innocent adults are being unjustly accused. The polarization among professionals is now so bad that researchers are quickly branded as being on one side or the other, and their work discounted by the opposition.

And both sides marshal horror stories as evidence. Read only one case of a child being treated for gonorrhea of the throat—the evidence that helped convict a man in Miami of child molestation—and you will feel a wave of nausea at what adults are capable of inflicting on children. Read only one false-accusation case, and you will feel misery and anger at what bureaucrats are capable of inflicting on parents. To further confuse the issue, the reality of the victimization of children is being obscured by a chorus of adults clamoring that they were victims too—if not as children, then as infants; if not in this life, then in a previous one. The evidence that abuse is more common than we knew is being trivialized by unvalidated claims made by pop-psychology writers that abuse is nearly universal, and that if you can't actually remember the abuse, that's all the more evidence that it happened to you.

Sexual-Abuse-Victim Stories

Women abused as children are indeed more likely than others to be depressed and to have low self-esteem as adults, although there is no good evidence from longitudinal studies showing that such abuse invariably causes the entire litany of women's problems. Nor does it follow that all women who are depressed, are sexually conflicted or wear baggy clothes were abused as children. Yet many are being encouraged to rifle their memories for clues that they were.

Thus E. Sue Blume: If you doubt you were abused, minimize the abuse or think "Maybe it's my imagination," these are symptoms of "post-incest syndrome."

And Ellen Bass and Laura Davis: "If you are unable to remember any specific instances . . . but still have a feeling that something abusive happened to you, it probably did. . . . If you think you were abused and your life shows the symptoms, then you were.". . .

And if a woman suspects that she has been abducted by U.F.O.'s, that the F.B.I. is bugging her socks or that a satanic cult forced her to bear a child that was half human and half dog, must she (and we) likewise assume that "it probably really happened"?

The sexual-abuse-victim story crystallizes many of society's anxieties about the vulnerability of children, the changing roles of women and the norms of sexuality. It draws like a magnet those who wish to invoke a measure of sympathy in these unsympathetic times. It is no wonder that publishers and talk shows have a thriving business exploiting stories of abuse for commercial reasons, for these are stories that sell. The childhood abuse explanation of all one's current problems, true or exaggerated, with or without the incest variation, is now de rigueur for any aspiring celebrity autobiographer (Patti Davis, Frances Lear, Suzanne Somers, Roseanne Arnold, La Toya Jackson).

As individual works of confession and advice, abuse-survivor books are often reassuring and supportive. They encourage victims of childhood molestation to speak up, to understand that they are not alone and to find help. The problem is not with the advice they offer to victims, but with their effort to create victims—to expand the market that can then be treated with therapy and self-help books. To do this, survival books all hew to a formula based on an uncritical acceptance of certain premises about the nature of memory and trauma. They offer simple answers at a time when research psychologists are posing hard questions.

THE POPULARITY OF REPRESSED MEMORY

To raise these questions does not mean that all "reawakened" memories are fraudulent or misguided. It does mean that we should be wary of believing every case of "me too!" that makes the news, and that we should be asking why these stories (and the advice books that play off them) are so popular now. We should also ask where these stories lead, with what consequences for individual well-being and social reform.

The great Swiss psychologist Jean Piaget once reported his earliest memory—nearly being kidnapped at the age of 2. Piaget remembered sitting in his baby carriage, watching his nurse defend him from the kidnapper. He remembered the scratches she had on her face. He remembered a police officer with a short cloak and a white baton who chased the kidnapper away. But none of it happened. When Piaget was 15, his former nurse wrote to his parents to confess that she had made up the entire story. Piaget wrote, "I therefore must have heard, as a child, the account of this story . . . and projected it into the past in the form of a visual memory, which was a memory of a memory, but false."

The harvest of incest-survivor books reflects the popular vision of mind and memory, in which the mind is a camera or tape recorder: all events that happen to us are recorded in memory, although trauma often causes them to be "repressed" until a significant event "unleashes" them and reveals at last what "actually" happened. This is a view of memory inspired partly by psychoanalysis and partly by contemporary metaphors of the mind, which historically have followed major inventions. Thus, during the Industrial Revolution, the brain was likened to a machine; after the invention of the telephone, to a switchboard; after the invention of movies, to a camera; after Univac, to a computer.

MEMORY IS NOT FIXED

Today many psychotherapists assume that everything significant that happens to us is imprinted somewhere in there, or maybe filed away in a dusty drawer (a metaphor for those of us who came of age before computers). Yet this view is increasingly at odds with that held by most academic psychologists. Researchers who study memory and the brain are discovering the brain's capacity to construct and invent reality from the information it processes. Their studies support what poets and novelists have always known: that memory is not a fixed thing, with its own special place or file drawer in the brain. It is a *process* that is constantly being reinvented. A "memory" consists of fragments of the event, subsequent discussions and reading, other people's recollections and suggestions, and, perhaps most of all, present beliefs about the past.

Thus, in the laboratory, the eminent memory researcher Elizabeth Loftus and her associates at the University of Washington have been able to inject false memories into people's minds by the mechanism of suggestion ("Remember when you were lost in that shopping mall at the age of 5?"). Similarly, the Canadian psychologist Nicholas P. Spanos and his team at Carleton University in Ottawa have created false memories of previous events and even of previous lives (at least in volunteers who believe in reincarnation). These scientists are finding that in the formation of a memory, current beliefs about past events are more important than what actually happened. This is why an event that seemed trivial when we were children can be reinterpreted and given new emotional significance when we are adults—and vice versa.

The mind does not record every detail of an event, but only a few features; we fill in the rest based on what "must have been." For an event to make it into long-term storage, a person has to perceive it, encode it and *rehearse* it—tell about it—or it decays. (This seems to be the major mechanism behind childhood amnesia, the fact that children do not develop long-term memory until roughly the age of 3.) Otherwise, research finds, even emotional experiences we are sure we will never forget—the Kennedy assassination, the Challenger explosion—will fade from memory, and errors will creep into the account that remains. . . .

Two recent books, scholarly yet highly readable, beautifully illuminate these complexities. In *Hidden Memories: Voices and Visions from Within*, Robert A. Baker, a retired professor of psychology who taught at the Massachusetts Institute of Technology, Stanford University and the University of Kentucky, reviews the research on the processes by which perfectly normal individuals can come to believe passionately that they were molested in the crib, abducted by U.F.O.'s or victimized by a satanic cult. And in *Trauma and Recovery*, Judith Lewis Herman, a psychiatrist who teaches at the Harvard Medical School, weaves together clinical and empirical evidence in exploring the nuances of trauma in all its varieties.

SCIENTIFIC EXPERTS OR WRITERS?

You would get none of this information or nuance, however, if you picked up any of the popular abuse-survivor books, such as *The Courage to Heal*. None of the authors are trained in research, which is not a comment on their ability to write or to do therapy, but which does seem to be one reason for their scientific illiteracy. The authors claim to be "experts" because (a) they were themselves molested, (b) they are social workers who treat incest victims in therapy, or (c) they wrote a book. Writing a book confers further expertise, because the authors then become "nationally recognized" lecturers who conduct workshops and train other psychotherapists. In what can only be called an Incestuous arrangement, the authors of these books all rely on one another's work as supporting evidence for their own; they all endorse and recommend one another's books to their readers. If one of them comes up with a concocted statistic—such as "more than half of all women are survivors of childhood sexual trauma"—the numbers are traded like baseball cards, reprinted in every book and eventually enshrined as fact. Thus the cycle of misinformation, faulty statistics and unvalidated assertions maintains itself. . . .

To reach their inflated statistics, the survivor books rely on definitions that are as expandable as a hot-air balloon. In these books, the rule is: If you feel abused, you were abused. According to the authors of *The Courage to Heal*, "Violation is determined by your experience as a child—your body, your feelings, your spirit. . . . Some abuse is not even physical." It doesn't matter if no sexual contact occurred; anything your parents did that you didn't like is a violation. Beverly Engel didn't like the way her mother would plant a "wet" kiss on her, look at her in ways that made her feel "queasy" and walk in on her in the bathroom. "It was not until very recently," she writes, "that I came to terms with my mother's behavior and saw it for what it really was— sexual abuse." This is a textbook example of the reconstructive nature of memory, showing how an adult belief can transform childhood experiences into "memories" of trauma.

FALSE MEMORIES

What is wrong with a therapist's belief in the "epidemic" prevalence of incest? Aren't we just quibbling about numbers, when the problem itself is real? Not to researchers such as Nicholas Spanos, who are worrying about the rise in what they call "pseudomemories" that are induced by some therapists and hypnotists—not only of incest, but also of past lives, multiple personalities and participation in satanic cults.

Mr. Spanos, who has conducted dozens of studies, has concluded that "suggestion-induced reports of perceptual and memory change" offered by hypnotized individuals should not be treated as actual descriptions of events. The "central component" in studies of hypnosis, he finds, is the willingness of hypnotized individuals "to bias their responses" as they believe the context demands.

Of course, all clients in therapy are influenced by the therapist's theoretical framework. This is why people in psychoanalysis have Freudian dreams, people in Jungian therapy have archetypal dreams, people in primal scream therapy remember being born and people in past-lives therapy remember being Julius Caesar (or whoever). Yet there is a sensitive line between any therapist's normal probing for evidence of certain psychological problems and literally creating them by the force of suggestion. Wendy Maltz and Beverly Holman, therapists in Eugene, Ore., make the process explicit in Incest and Sexuality: "It may take considerable digging on the part of the therapist," they say, "to discover incest as the source of the symptoms being experienced by the client." When does "considerable digging" become undue persuasion? On this subtle matter, the books are silent.

BLAMING PAST ABUSE FOR PRESENT TROUBLES

One other simplistic theme promulgated by the abuse-survivor books affects the survivors themselves and the solutions we seek, as a society, to the problem of childhood abuse. Uniformly, these books persuade their readers to focus exclusively on past abuse as the reason for their present unhappiness. Forget fighting with Harold and the kids, having a bad job or no job, worrying about money. Healing is *defined* as your realization that you were a victim of sexual abuse and that it explains everything wrong in your life.

'You just think you're suffering from false memory syndrome.'

Reprinted by permission of the *Spectator*, London.

Beverly Engel even offers a list of stages in which the victim proceeds from darkness into light. In the first stage, she, like "many victims of childhood sexual abuse," has no conscious memory of having been abused, so she denies her symptoms. In the next stage, visiting a therapist or reading one of these books, she begins to suspect she was abused. In the third stage, she still doesn't know that she is a victim because she doesn't realize that what happened to her was abuse. In the fourth stage, she knows she was sexually abused but fails to connect her "symptoms" with the abuse. In the last stage of healing, she knows she was abused and connects the dots to her present unhappiness.

You can see this process at work in Betsy Petersen's *Dancing with Daddy: A Childhood Lost and a Life Regained* (1991). According to Ms. Petersen, the incest (which she never actually remembers) explained her nightmares, eating disorders, compulsive cleanliness, shame about sexuality, anxieties, drive for self-improvement, colon problems, back pain, insecurity about money, difficulties in wishing for something for herself, impatience with the obnoxious behavior of her sons, and even why she cooked a hot breakfast for her dogs every morning. It explained, as if no other woman had this problem, her vulnerability to fad diets. It explained, as if no other new parent had this problem, her awkwardness with her firstborn son. It explained, as if no other modern adult had this problem, her malaise of alienation and loneliness.

For Ms. Petersen, all current events are processed through the lens of incest. "Before I knew my father had molested me," she says, "the feelings cycled endlessly and attached themselves to the world outside my skin: If only my children weren't so demanding, I would think, I wouldn't feel so crazy." Exactly! One day her son, whining to be taken out for fast food, screamed and cursed her, and threw his shoe. She writes: "And suddenly I was *so mad*. My stomach hurt." Was she angry about this behavior? Oh, no; she was, angry *at her father*.

THERAPY DOES NOT CREATE SOCIAL CHANGE

Betsy Petersen seems to have completely shut out "the world outside my skin," and ultimately that is the problem and the appeal of the survivor narrative. It places responsibility for the common problems in women's lives on a single clear villain, someone safely in the woman's past. The victim doesn't have to do anything except understand the origins of her problems. Her partner doesn't have to change, as long as he is sympathetic to her early trauma. And she gets a love bath from her friends and supporters. Who could resist? In this respect, the sexual-survivor narrative, like other popular theories based on female psyche and biology, locates the origins of women's victimization, powerlessness and unhappiness inside the woman. It's in her; it's up to her to fix herself.

In 1978, Louise Armstrong wrote one of the first incest-survivor books, *Kiss Daddy Goodnight*. To Ms. Armstrong and other feminist writers, incest and other forms of child abuse were not the aberrations of a few sick men, but the results of a system that endows men with the sense of entitlement to own and abuse women and children. Today the survivor movement has shifted from an emphasis on social change to one on psychological solace. Reflecting in a revised edition of her book on how public conversation about incest changed in the decade since its publication, Ms. Armstrong mused: "Where is everybody? I sometimes ask, meaning the survivors. The voices of no-nonsense, unsentimental, unromantic reason. Oh (the answer comes back), they're in therapy. Nothing wrong with that. We all need help and support." But, she continued, "exclusively personal solutions do nothing to defy the ongoing tacit permission for abuse."

Contemporary incest-survivor books encourage women to incorporate the language of victimhood and survival into the sole organizing narrative of their identity. It becomes their major story, and its moral rarely goes farther than "Join a group and talk about your feelings." Such stories soothe women temporarily while allowing everyone else to go free. That is why these stories are so popular. If the victim can fix herself, nothing has to change.

"This is the first time in history that children and adults who were sexually abused have been listened to, respected, and believed."

INCEST SURVIVORS DESERVE SUPPORT AND RESPECT

Ellen Bass and Laura Davis

Adults who suffered sexual abuse as children should be supported and believed, argue Ellen Bass and Laura Davis in the following viewpoint. Although critics have claimed that therapists and support groups encourage people to invent memories of childhood sexual abuse, the authors contend, these attacks have failed to prove that such memories are fabricated. In fact, Bass and Davis maintain, those who challenge the credibility of survivors' experiences are part of a backlash rooted in America's chronic denial about the realities of childhood sexual abuse. The survivor movement both encourages individual healing from past abuse and promotes social activism to reduce sexual violence, the authors assert. Bass and Davis are the authors of The Courage to Heal: A Guide for Women Survivors of Child Sexual Abuse, from which this viewpoint is excerpted.

As you read, consider the following questions:

1. According to Bass and Davis, how have survivors of childhood sexual abuse been affected by the backlash against the incest-survivor movement?
2. How were accounts of childhood sexual abuse addressed before the 1980s, according to the authors?
3. In the authors' opinion, what three elements are typically present when incest survivors recall previously blocked memories of sexual abuse?

S ince 1992 we have watched with growing concern the emerging backlash against survivors of child sexual abuse, their supporters, and the significant social progress they have made. There has been a barrage of articles, magazine stories, and radio and TV talk shows that have attacked the credibility of sexual abuse survivors, their therapists, and support books such as *The Courage to Heal*. Headlines like "Repressed Memories, Ruined Lives," "Beware the Incest Survivor Machine," and "When Memory Holds a Family Hostage" have appeared in newspapers across the country. . . .

Many of those who challenge the credibility of survivors claim that recovered memories of child sexual abuse are untrue, that substantial numbers of people are falsely accused, and that those who say they are survivors often have been misled—or even brainwashed—by naive or manipulative therapists, authors, and book publishers.

Initially we thought the wisest response was to ignore these attacks, that the obvious truth of child sexual abuse would prevail. But to our dismay, highly biased stories, lacking in historical context or political analysis, kept appearing in major newspapers across the country. Story after story passed off nearly identical quotes, distortions, and misinformation as fact. The Courage to Heal and other books were quoted out of context. Studies on the nature of memory were misrepresented. Extreme cases of abuse were presented as the norm so as to provoke disbelief about child sexual abuse. And stories of family strife were almost always told from the perspective of the people accused.

Most of the coverage has been extremely adversarial, belittling survivors, depicting them as gullible victims, vengeful children, or simply crazy. Unfortunately, survivors have heard this all too often.

As the backlash became a major media event, we began to hear from survivors, many of them alarmed by this nationwide assault on their integrity. . . .

THE IMPACT ON SURVIVORS

Many survivors have been concerned about the impact this public wave of denial will have on their healing. They've expressed how excruciating it is to have their hard work in healing—and in changing the attitudes in our culture—undermined. One woman said:

> The attacks being made on survivors and those who help them really scare me. It is frightening to think that therapists and people who help survivors could come under such pressure—legal and otherwise—that they would no longer be able to provide their services. It feels like a real war.

And another:

> The recent surge of attacks may cause an untold number of survivors to continue to suffer in silence, thereby protecting their abusers . . . and effectively perpetuating the already out-of-control cycle of abuse in this country.

. . . It was because of letters like these, and out of concern for the impact of this backlash on all survivors, that we decided to respond. . . .

A HISTORY OF DENIAL

Until the 1980s, emerging accounts of child sexual abuse were met primarily with denial, minimization, and blaming the victim. In the first three-quarters of the twentieth century, sexual abuse was primarily considered the fault of the child. In 1907 Karl Abraham described a nine-year-old girl who had been led into the woods by a neighbor who then attempted to rape her. The child fought off the man and managed to run away, but Abraham wrote that she had "allowed herself to be seduced" and had "allowed him to go a long way in carrying out his purpose before she freed herself from him and ran off. It's not to be wondered at that this child kept the occurrence secret."

In 1937 Loretta Bender and Adam Blau wrote, "These children undoubtedly do not deserve completely the cloak of innocence with which they have been endowed by moralists, social reformers and legislators." Referring to the children's "unusually charming and attractive . . . personalities," they went on to conclude that "the child might have been the actual seducer rather than the one innocently seduced."

And in 1953, Alfred Kinsey and his fellow researchers documented the prevalence of child sexual abuse but minimized its impact. In a sample of over one thousand women, one in four reported sexual abuse. Eighty percent of these said they had been frightened by the encounters, but Kinsey and his colleagues discounted their accounts, writing, "It is difficult to understand why a child, except for its cultural conditioning, should be disturbed at having its genitalia touched." They went on to express their belief that penalties for perpetrators were overly harsh: "In many instances the law, in the course of punishing the offender, does more damage to more persons than was ever done by the individual in his illicit sexual activity.". . .

Interestingly, while some professionals were blaming everyone but the perpetrator, others were insisting that child sexual abuse didn't happen at all—or only very rarely. As late as the

1970s many clinicians were still taught that incest was extremely rare, affecting only one in a million children.

Considering this history, our present ability to recognize and confront child sexual abuse is nothing short of phenomenal.

The advances of the past twenty years are a direct outgrowth of the women's liberation movement that gained force in the 1970s. Women courageously spoke out about rape and battering, wrote books analyzing the ways in which our society condoned such violence, and worked to establish battered women's shelters and rape crisis centers. Simultaneously, a few pioneering clinicians and researchers, both men and women, were beginning to study child sexual abuse and set up models for treatment. It was from this visionary thinking—grassroots activism—that the current movement to end child sexual abuse was built.

We began to insist that children be protected, survivors be supported, and perpetrators be held responsible for their acts. This monumental advance in our willingness to be aware, to care, and to respond has come about only in the past two decades—most visibly in the past decade. This is the first time in history that children and adults who were sexually abused have been listened to, respected, and believed.

Adult survivors of child sexual abuse now have a voice and the power of community. Survivors are educating the medical profession, mental health workers, teachers, law enforcement officers, and the media. Laws are being changed. As a nation we are stunned to learn that our children are being harmed in great numbers. We have begun to break through our collective wall of denial—a wall that has been at least as hard as the Berlin Wall to bring down. This is revolutionary change, and such change does not come without opposition.

There is a documented history of backlash against every progressive movement to redress the rights of the disenfranchised and oppressed. No significant steps are won without it. Although the attacks on survivors of child sexual abuse are extremely upsetting, they are also an indication of the substantial social progress we have made. Our movement has attained sufficient momentum, visibility, and clout to attract such opposition.

The current backlash is in direct response to the activism of survivors. It was not until survivors started challenging and changing the laws regarding the accountability of perpetrators—and suing their abusers—that claims of "false memory syndrome" started to appear.

And this denial, although it has a new name and a new face,

is really the same old thing. Judith Herman, associate clinical professor of psychiatry at Harvard Medical School, explains:

> For the past twenty years, women have been speaking out about sexual violence, and men have been coming up with denials, evasions, and excuses. We have been told that women lie, exaggerate, and fantasize. Now [we're being told] that women are brainwashed. . . . Once again, those of us who have labored for years to overcome public denial find ourselves debating victims' credibility. How many times do we have to go over the same ground? . . .

The Truth About Recovering Memories

It is unusual for therapists to convince their clients that abuse took place when it didn't.

The core of the "false memory" argument is that fictitious memories of child sexual abuse are implanted in the minds of impressionable patients by overeager, manipulative, or greedy therapists, and that they use coercive mind-control techniques to do so.

This is not how responsible therapists work. The foundation of good therapy is a respectful relationship in which the therapist provides a safe space, genuine caring, and support. Good therapists don't lead—they follow their clients into the difficult and painful places they need to go. In doing so, their clients are empowered to do their own healing work, to uncover their own history, to find their own truth. As Judith Herman explains, "Psychotherapy is a collaborative effort, not a form of totalitarian indoctrination."

If it were really possible for therapists to create new memories in their clients, survivors of child sexual abuse would, in fact, probably be the first to sign up. As one survivor put it, "If it is so common and so easily accomplished to alter or even implant memories, where can I get some new ones? Mine are all too real and sickening and frankly, I'm tired of them."

This is not to say that there aren't bad or even abusive therapists. Unethical therapists have forced hospitalizations, overmedicated their patients, had sex with clients, and perpetrated a variety of other abuses. But such practitioners are not representative of the mental health profession as a whole. . . .

Many Survivors Recall Abuse Without Therapy

Therapy is rarely the sole or primary trigger for memories of child sexual abuse.

Proponents of the "false memory syndrome" promote the belief that most adult survivors regain their memories of child sexual abuse at the instigation of a therapist. This is not true. Many survivors never see a therapist at all. They struggle along as best they can without coming to terms with the abuse, or they work through their pain without the aid of a counselor. Of those who do seek therapy, many already know about the abuse. Either they've always remembered it and they now are ready to seek help, or something else has triggered the memories and they need help coping with the fallout.

There are three factors that are usually present when adults (or adolescents) recall abuse they have previously blocked out: distance from the original abuse, a life circumstance that leads to the letting down of normal defenses, and an external event that restimulates the memory. These factors can exist in a good therapeutic relationship, and therefore some survivors do uncover abuse while in therapy. But recall of child sexual abuse is far more common in other circumstances.

Life transitions—puberty, childbirth, a commitment to an intimate relationship, the death of a parent, retirement, moving, menopause, aging, divorce, losses of any kind—frequently trigger memories. So does sobriety. Medical treatment—a trip to the dentist, an exam by a gynecologist or urologist, surgery or other invasive medical procedures—can also jar loose buried feelings and images. Adult experiences of victimization—a rape, a robbery, being fired from a job—often stir up memories of earlier violations. Parents sometimes remember their own abuse when their child is abused or when that child reaches the age they were when they were first abused. Survivors may also remember while making love, exercising, or getting massaged—when they use their bodies in a new way.

Of course any of these life events may occur while a survivor is in therapy. And a survivor may seek therapy for help in coping with such events. But a therapist's question, or even suggestion, about sexual abuse is rarely the only or most significant reason for memories to emerge.

CHRONIC TRAUMA CREATES MULTIPLE SYMPTOMS

There is a lot more to determining whether someone is a survivor than a single memory.

The "false memory" argument hinges on the assumption that an assessment of child sexual abuse is based solely or primarily on memory. But that isn't true. Long-term trauma is reflected in the daily lives of many survivors. For some the injury is obvious—they have suffered from severe and debilitating symptoms for many years. Some have permanent physical damage that is unmistakably traumatic in origin. Other survivors have been successful at creating highly functional lives, but their inner world is self-hating or full of pain. These effects, which have frequently been present for years prior to uncovering a sexual abuse history, are not created in a therapist's office.

Reconstructing a history of child sexual abuse is a complex process based on a whole constellation of symptoms, of which memory is just a part. Phobias, flashbacks, intrusive imagery, chronic patterns of denial and dissociation, flooding of feelings, spontaneous regression, startle reflexes, numbness in the body, and terror of sex may all point to a history of trauma in childhood.

Those who say memories of sexual abuse can be implanted fail to explain the presence of these symptoms. A therapist cannot induce you to jump out of your skin every time someone comes up behind you. "False memories" cannot explain why you see your abuser's face when you climax, why you're terrified of subway cars, why you carve into your body, or why you wake up terrified every morning at 4:00 a.m. These and hundreds of other distressing patterns fall through the cracks of the "false memory" theory and are, unfortunately, often explained by an all-too-real history of child sexual abuse. . . .

LISTENING TO SURVIVORS

The strides we've made in recognizing and dealing with child sexual abuse in the past fifteen years have been both positive and far-reaching. As a society we have begun to assert the right of children to grow up free from battering, emotional abuse, and sexual terrorism. We have challenged the status quo—children as property—and as a result, our hard-fought gains are being attacked. The current backlash against survivors of child sexual abuse is a destructive, undermining force, and the use of that force has been intentional.

We are at a crossroads. As a society we can continue to fight for the integrity of every child and the healing of every survivor, or we can give in to our collective denial and once again bury the truth. . . .

We must reaffirm that survivors of child sexual abuse are the true experts on their experience. Many professionals have spoken out eloquently on behalf of survivors—and many others have insulted, pathologized, or dismissed them. Yet in the midst of all this debate *about* survivors, we need to remember that our greatest understanding comes not in listening to professionals, but to the survivors themselves.

"Some battered women have used up all their choices and have none left. Sometimes these women kill. Juries ought to hear why."

BATTERED WOMAN SYNDROME IS A VALID DEFENSE

Abbe Smith

Battered woman syndrome is the psychological state suffered by women who fear they will be killed by their abusive spouses if they try to leave the relationship. Many psychologists and legal experts claim that women who kill their abusive husbands suffer from battered woman syndrome and see murder as the only option available to them. In the following viewpoint, criminal defense lawyer Abbe Smith argues that battered woman syndrome is a valid defense in criminal cases involving abused women who have killed their male partners. In her opinion, female murder defendants suffering from this syndrome should receive the same kind of consideration given to men who kill in self-defense.

As you read, consider the following questions:

1. In Smith's opinion, what presumption does society impose on battered women?
2. According to the author, on what occasion did the U.S. government act in retaliatory self-defense?
3. In the author's opinion, why is the phrase "battered woman" inaccurate?

Excerpted from Abbe Smith, "Criminal Responsibility, Social Responsibility, and Angry Young Men: Reflections of a Feminist Criminal Defense Lawyer," *N.Y.U. Review of Law and Social Change*, vol. 21, no. 3, 1994–1995. Reprinted with permission.

He beat me like he beat the children. 'Cept he don't never hardly beat them. He say, Celie, git the belt. The children be outside the room peeking through the cracks. It all I can do not to cry. I make myself wood. I say to myself, Celie, you a tree.

—Alice Walker, *The Color Purple*

Her dress it was a snowy white
A rose tied to her wrist
The words her daddy preached to her
Were softened with a kiss
They'll judge you by your company
They cannot see beyond
Be careful who you choose in life
And stay where you belong

—Kate and Anna McGarrigle, "Leave Me Be"

Battered women who become criminal defendants are punished long before the question of responsibility is addressed. They're physically abused, psychologically tormented, sexually assaulted, and then arrested and prosecuted. The system functions like something out of *Alice in Wonderland*: they're punished first, then tried, and then sentenced.

SOCIETAL CONDEMNATION

The central problem with battered women's self-defense cases is that society imposes on these women an especially powerful presumption of choice. Once women make a romantic choice, they must literally live (or die) with it, as the above song by Kate and Anna McGarrigle suggests. Society attributes a number of choices to battered women who kill: first they choose the wrong guy, then they choose to marry (or live with or date) him, then they choose to be beaten (or accept it or fail to successfully resist it), then they choose to stay, and then they choose to kill him. Some jurors may think the killing was the worst choice; others may condemn her most for staying.

When a battered woman kills and claims self-defense, she is often held responsible for her original "choice" in men. A litany of culture-driven clichés rain upon the defendant: She made her bed, now let her lie in it. She didn't try hard enough to get away. She should have left him. She didn't go through the proper channels.

The chief legal obstacle for women who claim self-defense after killing their abusers is establishing the element of imminent danger. Somehow, the way women kill never quite comports with prevailing notions of appropriate self-protection. In the words of Abigail Trafford:

> Killing in self-defense is a fundamental right for men and nations. . . . But when women kill their husbands because they are afraid for their lives and those of their children, it's considered shocking—and criminal. According to the popular myth, a wan, mousy wife suddenly loses it and kills the hapless guy in his sleep. Or she hires a friend to blow him away and stuffs his body in a garbage can. It's all very weird and female.

JUSTIFIABLE SELF-DEFENSE

In 1993, the United States launched missiles to attack Iraq. It claimed the action was justifiable self-defense under the United Nations Charter, because it learned of an alleged Iraqi plot to assassinate former President George Bush six months before. Even though the United States *waited* for "certain proof" before striking, nobody had problems with this sort of self-defense, or with the lack of imminent danger. Retaliatory self-defense is somehow not a contradiction in terms for the United States government.

© Kirk Anderson. Reprinted with permission.

The reaction is different when it comes to women who kill their batterers, whether or not they kill in the course of a confrontation and when the danger is most imminent. The only time battered women seem to draw wide public support and approval is when they die at the hands of their abusers. Only then do people lament, "Gee, she was telling the truth, she really *was* in danger." When the man is the dead one, though, suddenly no one is sure.

"BATTERING MEN SYNDROME"

I must confess that I am not crazy about the term "battered woman." I do not want to think of women who are assaulted by men as a psychological subgroup of "normal" women. We do not think of people assaulted on the street as a psychological subgroup of "normal" people. I think "battered women's syndrome" makes the women being beaten sound like the sick ones, rather than the men who are doing the beating. Although child abuse and elder abuse conjure images of nasty perpetrators preying on innocent victims, spousal abuse conjures images of pathetic, masochistic women, suffering from, at best, a "syndrome." Why do we hold battered women responsible for being beaten? Why do we think there's a difference between women who defend themselves against men with whom they have been intimate and women who defend themselves against relative strangers? Maybe it has something to do with the mythology of love. We think that women whom men have "loved" have the power to make things better. The existence of some sort of "love" relationship suggests the possibility of reconciliation, even redemption. Or maybe we think that women bring these things upon themselves.

I think the onus should be on the batterers, not the battered: we should investigate the existence of a battering men syndrome. The problem, of course, is that the battering men syndrome, a product of cultural socialization and individual disorder, will probably never make it into the DSM IV (*Diagnostic and Statistical Manual of Mental Disorders*, 4th ed.].

THE SPECTRUM OF CHOICES

I feel the same way about the capacity of abused women to choose to kill as I do about choice in general: it lies somewhere on a spectrum. Some battered women have more choices than others. Some battered women have some choices but not others. Some battered women have some choices, sometimes. Some battered women have used up all their choices and have none left. Sometimes these women kill. Juries ought to hear why.

| "When killing a man in his sleep can be justified as self-defense, it seems like a prescription for legalized murder."

BATTERED WOMAN SYNDROME IS RARELY A VALID DEFENSE

Michael Weiss and Cathy Young

Battered woman syndrome has been used as trial evidence by women who claim that killing their husbands was the only way they could escape ongoing and life-threatening spousal abuse. In the following viewpoint, Michael Weiss and Cathy Young contend that "battering" has become so broadly defined that psychological abuse and neglect are now considered forms of spousal abuse. Because of this expanded definition of abuse, the authors argue, many women who murdered their husbands out of anger or revenge have received acquittals by using the battered-woman defense. Since previously established self-defense laws already protect defendants who kill to save their lives, battered woman syndrome should rarely be allowed as trial evidence, the authors conclude. Michael Weiss is a professor at the University of Houston Law Center and a fellow at the Texas Public Policy Foundation. Cathy Young is an associate policy analyst for the Cato Institute, a libertarian research foundation.

As you read, consider the following questions:

1. According to the authors, how does the New Jersey Supreme Court define battered woman syndrome?
2. What proof was traditionally required for self-defense pleas in murder trials, according to Weiss and Young?
3. How do the cases cited by Coramae Richey Mann illustrate the misuse of battered woman syndrome, in the authors' opinion?

Excerpted from Michael Weiss and Cathy Young, "Feminist Jurisprudence: Equal Rights or Neo-Paternalism?" *Cato Institute Policy Analysis*, no. 256, June 19, 1996. Reprinted by permission of the Cato Institute.

The first steps toward the implementation of feminist jurisprudence on a national scale have taken place in Canada, though not without assistance from American feminists. . . .

One American feminist who wields great influence in Canada is Lenore Walker, whose role in pioneering the "battered wife syndrome" was commended by the Canadian Supreme Court in a key 1990 decision upholding that defense. . . .

To Lenore Walker, members of the patriarchy's ruling class not only are not entitled to traditional civil rights but, in some cases, are not entitled to live. A psychologist, legal theorist, and director of the Domestic Violence Institute, Walker is the leading exponent of the battered woman syndrome. She makes no secret of the ideological nature of her work:

> A feminist political gender analysis has reframed the problem of violence against women as one of misuse of power by men who have been socialized into believing they have the right to control the women in their lives, even through violent means. . . . [T]he underbelly of interpersonal violence is seen as the socialized androcentric need for power. Feminists believe that violence against women is at the core of all violence in the world.

In her 1979 book *The Battered Woman*, Walker defines the elements of the battered woman syndrome: "A battered woman is a woman who is repeatedly subjected to any forceful physical or psychological behavior by a man in order to coerce her to do something he wants her to do without any concern for her rights. . . . To be classified as a battered woman, the couple must go through the battering cycle at least twice."

BATTERING IS DEFINED TOO BROADLY

Walker makes it clear that a woman can be "battered" even if there is no physical violence: "I decided that a woman's story was to be accepted if she felt she was being psychologically and/or physically battered by her man." In the case of one couple Walker profiles, she acknowledges that the wife clearly initiated the physical assault, throwing a glass at her husband's head and hitting him with a chair, but adds that "it is also clear from the rest of her story that Paul had been battering her by ignoring her and by working late, in order to move up the corporate ladder, for the entire five years of their marriage."

When battering is defined so broadly and so vaguely, it is hardly surprising that Walker finds it to be quite common: "Our research and most other studies show that wife-battering occurs in 50 percent of families throughout the nation." Walker believes that virtually every woman who kills her mate is a victim of the battered woman syndrome. As the New Jersey Supreme Court (echoing Walker) described the condition, battered women "become so demoralized and degraded by the fact that they cannot predict or control the violence that they sink into a state of psychological paralysis and become unable to take any action at all to improve or alter the situation" short of killing the abuser. . . .

CLAIMS OF SELF-DEFENSE

In the 1970s and early 1980s, women charged with murdering their alleged batterers began to assert self-defense claims based on the battered woman syndrome. The first question faced by state courts was whether expert testimony on the syndrome was admissible. In 1979, the first decision allowing such testimony came down from the District of Columbia Circuit Court of Appeals. Since then, appellate courts in 26 states have addressed the issue. Seventeen states have concluded that expert testimony on the battered woman syndrome is admissible; only three exclude it.

Traditionally in the Anglo-American system, those pleading self-defense in murder trials had to prove that they faced imminent danger at the time of killing with no means of escape. In other words, they had to show that they had been fending off an actual attack and had had to use force to do so. Once the aggressor made a move to retreat, the defense of self-defense was no longer available.

PARDONS FOR HUSBAND KILLERS

There have been no mass pardons of wife killers as there have been of husband killers in both Ohio and Maryland. One of the Maryland women freed had hired a hit man and collected on her husband's insurance policy. The Columbus (Ohio) Dispatch reported that of the 25 women pardoned by outgoing governor Richard Celeste in 1990, 15 said they had not been physically abused. Six had discussed killing their husbands beforehand, and 2 had even tracked down their estranged spouses to kill them.

Battered woman syndrome is simply a sign of the times. In a nation of victims, everything can be justified on the basis of abuse of some sort.

Michael Fumento, Insight, February 6, 1995.

Proponents of the battered-woman defense claim that existing legal doctrine "is defined in a narrow and male-identified fashion to encompass . . . encounters between men of roughly equal size and strength" and "refuses to take into account the social context of a battered-woman defendant's act."

In fact, as New York University law professor Holly Maguigan (who is sympathetic to the battered-woman defense) acknowledges, traditional self-defense law does not exclude the context of the event, such as previous threats or assaults. In 1902, long before battered woman syndrome was born, the Texas Court of Criminal Appeals reversed a woman's conviction for killing her husband because evidence of past violence had been excluded from the trial:

> [I]t is admissible for the defendant, having first established that she was . . . in apparent danger, to prove that the deceased was a person of ferocity [and] excessive strength . . . for the purpose of showing either (1) that the defendant was acting in terror, and hence incapable of that specific malice necessary to constitute murder in the first degree; or (2) that she was in such apparent extremity as to make out a case of self-defense.

SELF-DEFENSE LAW ALREADY PROTECTS WOMEN

In other spousal homicide cases in the pre-feminist 1940s, 1950s, and 1960s, appellate courts held that such factors as prior abuse and differences in physical strength needed to be considered to determine whether the defendant was reasonably responding in proportion to the threat. If, as Maguigan argues, the law is often not applied fairly in cases of this kind, that is no reason to overhaul the basic premises of self-defense law.

The battered-woman defense seeks to establish the possibility of self-defense in cases where, even with such factors as prior violence or differences in strength taken into account, no court would have made such a finding under traditional doctrine. In 1981, Janice Leidholm stabbed her husband Chester to death as he slept after an argument that involved yelling and shoving; the marriage had a history of violence. Under legal precedent, evidence of past abuse should have been inadmissible because it could have no bearing on whether Leidholm was in imminent danger. (She clearly was not, with her husband asleep.) Yet the judge allowed prior abuse into evidence and instructed the jury on self-defense. When Leidholm was found guilty nonetheless, the North Dakota Supreme Court threw out the conviction on the grounds that the judge had told the jury to consider whether she had acted justifiably by the standard of a person "of ordinary prudence and circumspection," rather than by her own subjective standards. When killing a man in his sleep can be justified as self-defense, it seems like a prescription for legalized murder. . . .

Other cases are never even tried. Reviewing a sample of

female-offender homicides, sociologist Coramae Richey Mann found the case of a woman who claimed self-defense after shooting her husband six times in the back of the head in a domestic argument during which he had threatened her with a chair. The case was dismissed. In Brooklyn, New York, in 1987, Marlene Wagshall shot her sleeping husband in the stomach with a .357 magnum revolver after finding a photo of him with another woman. (He survived but lost parts of his stomach, liver, and upper intestine.) There was no evidence to corroborate her claims of physical abuse. A grand jury indicted Wagshall for attempted murder, but feminist District Attorney Elizabeth Holtzman reduced the charge to second-degree assault and accepted a guilty plea with a sentence of one day in jail and five years' probation.

DIFFERENT LAWS FOR MEN AND WOMEN?

In a speech in Banff, Canada, Andrea Dworkin exhorted her audience to "stop men who beat women": "Get them jailed or get them killed. . . . When the law fails us, we cannot fail each other." The exhortation to break the law if it cannot be tailored to the radical feminist program shows the lengths to which the activists are willing to travel to implement their vision of a redistribution of power. Instead of focusing on measures to prevent and punish domestic assault no matter who commits it—a need to which police, courts, and social agencies should be more responsive—they seek to have one set of laws for women and another for men. What is alarming is that, all too often, the courts are helping in this endeavor.

In some spousal homicide cases, a history of past violence and especially threats to the person's life may undoubtedly be relevant to a finding of self-defense. Here, expert opinion on spousal abuse may have a place in the courtroom. Nonetheless, the concept of the battered woman syndrome needs to be reexamined impartially, given clear evidence that this condition was originally formulated on the basis of political rather than scientific premises.

PERIODICAL BIBLIOGRAPHY

The following articles have been selected to supplement the diverse views presented in this chapter. Addresses are provided for periodicals not indexed in the *Readers' Guide to Periodical Literature*, the *Alternative Press Index*, the *Social Sciences Index*, or the *Index to Legal Periodicals and Books*.

Carol J. Adams	"Help for the Battered," *Christian Century*, June 29–July 6, 1994.
Linda Crockett	"Companions of Comfort: A Healing for Survivors of Sexual Abuse and War," *Sojourners*, July/August 1995.
Jean Bethke Elshtain	"Women and the Ideology of Victimization," *World & I*, April 1993.
David Frum	"Women Who Kill," *Forbes*, January 18, 1993.
Christine Gorman	"Memory on Trial," *Time*, April 17, 1995.
Michele Ingrassia and Melinda Beck	"Patterns of Abuse," *Newsweek*, July 4, 1994.
Cindi Leive	"The Final Rape Injustice," *Glamour*, November 1994.
Rich Lowry	"Creating Victims," *National Review*, December 5, 1994.
Mary Nemeth and William Lowther	"Judgment Day," *Maclean's*, January 31, 1994.
Mark Pendergrast	"Remembering the Past: A New Chapter in the Old Story of Women and Oppression," *Omni*, February 1995.
Anna Quindlen	"After the Rape," *New York Times*, October 19, 1994.
Julia Reed	"Excuse Me," *Vogue*, May 1994.
Suzanne Rotondo	"Who's Protecting Whom?" *Peace Review*, vol. 7, nos. 3/4, 1995.
C. SerVaas	"Easing Woes for Rape Victims," *Saturday Evening Post*, May/June 1993.
Natalia Rachel Singer	"Journey to Justice," *Ms.*, November/December 1994.
John Taylor	"The Lost Daughter," *Esquire*, March 1994.
Ruth Wallen	"Memory Politics: The Implications of Healing from Sexual Abuse," *Tikkun*, November/December 1994.
Teresa Yunker	"When Street Harassment Gets Nasty," *On the Issues*, Summer 1996.

CHAPTER 4

HOW CAN SEXUAL
VIOLENCE BE REDUCED?

CHAPTER PREFACE

Richard and Maureen Kanka's seven-year-old daughter, Megan, was raped and murdered in Hamilton, New Jersey, in 1994. The Kankas were infuriated when they discovered that the man accused of killing Megan was a twice-convicted child molester who had moved in across the street from their home. Their outrage led to the adoption of a state law—and in 1996 a federal law—known as "Megan's Law," which requires local police to notify communities when convicted sex offenders move into the neighborhood.

Critics of Megan's Law maintain that such notification laws constitute an invasion of privacy and are unconstitutional because they impose punishments on people who have already served their sentences. For example, Alexander Artway, who served seventeen years for sexual assault, filed suit in New Jersey, claiming that the state's disclosure of his sex-offender status is punitive and violates his constitutional rights.

New Jersey's attorney general has defended the constitutionality of Megan's Law, with mixed results. In February 1995 the Third Circuit Court ruled in *Artway v. Attorney General* that the state law does not violate a convicted sex offender's right to privacy because much of the information disseminated is publicly available. And although the registration requirement may have a "branding" effect, the court ruled that it is permissible because it serves to combat a high rate of recidivism among released sex offenders. However, the Third Circuit Court also declared that because the public notification provisions of Megan's Law can affect the offender's employability and business and social relationships, they are punitive and therefore unconstitutional. The attorney general's office appealed the ruling on the notification provisions to the U.S. Court of Appeals and, as of December 1996, is awaiting a decision.

Community registration and notification laws may violate the rights of sexual offenders; not registering the offenders and notifying the public may endanger the public. The authors in the following chapter debate these hard choices as they examine ways to reduce sexual violence.

"In conjunction with psychological counseling, most testosterone-lowering treatments are effective."

CASTRATION OF SEX OFFENDERS WOULD REDUCE SEXUAL VIOLENCE

Larry Don McQuay and Fred S. Berlin

In Part I of the following two-part viewpoint, convicted child molester Larry Don McQuay maintains that the fear of being sent to prison after his release will not deter him from molesting children again. He contends that castration is the only treatment that will keep him from molesting children. In Part II, Fred S. Berlin asserts that chemical castration—injections of a female hormone that reduce a man's sexual desire—is an effective treatment for sex offenders, especially when used together with psychological counseling. Berlin is an associate professor at the Johns Hopkins University School of Medicine and the director of the National Institute for the Study, Prevention and Treatment of Sexual Trauma.

As you read, consider the following questions:

1. In McQuay's view, why are prisons a failure at curing child molesters of their desires?
2. How do the recidivism rates compare for sex offenders who do not receive treatment and for those who do, according to the Swiss study cited by Berlin?
3. What is the precedent Berlin cites for compelling sex offenders to involuntarily undergo castration?

From Larry Don McQuay, "The Case for Castration, Part 1" and Fred S. Berlin, "The Case for Castration, Part 2," *Washington Monthly*, May 1994. Reprinted by permission of the publisher.

I

Children's nightmares are haunted by demons, some imagined, others real. I'm one of the real ones; I haunt the dreams of scores of children. You'll find me in a Texas prison serving an eight year sentence for molesting a single boy. That's all the court convicted me of, but I have abused close to 200 children.

In the United States, thousands of kids meet monsters like me each year. We prowl your communities, stalking, pouncing when possible, forcing children to endure degrading, violent acts. We wear the innocent-looking masks of a father, step-father, uncle, cousin. We could wear the caring face of a baby-sitter, or a teacher, or a priest. I myself have worn various masks: brother, cousin, step-father, uncle, school-bus driver, family friend. All to molest unsuspecting boys and girls.

Scarcely a week goes by without another disturbing news report about another poor soul victimized by a child rapist. Listen carefully to that next report. Odds are that you'll hear that this same sex offender had a past conviction for molesting at least one other child.

Prison Is Not a Deterrent

That's because prison is not a deterrent for most sex offenders, and it definitely will not be a deterrent for me. I do not want to return to prison; I would like to be a law abiding citizen. But the threat of being incarcerated for the rest of my life—and the threat of spending, as I believe I will, an eternity in hell—will not stop me from re-offending when I am released.

In fact, in many cases, prison intensifies sex offenders' conditions by making us more savage. Where once we would "play-fully" undress a victim, we now roughly strip them. What was once inappropriate touching and "caressing" escalates to a full-scale invasion. What was fondling and masturbation becomes dehumanizing sodomy. What used to be a cultivated "relation-ship" that took time and preparation becomes an unplanned kidnapping and rape where children are beaten, tortured, ravaged, and often found dead and mutilated, or never found at all. You see, sex offenders who've been to prison not only emerge with an appetite for violence but also learn a lesson about how to stay out of jail: make sure that the next victim can't *ever* report them.

I speak from experience. Lately, many of my dreams and fantasies have become more violent. My sleep is plagued with fantasies of raping kidnapped children in a way that renders them unable to identify me. Without the right treatment, I believe that eventually I will rape, then murder, my victims to keep them from reporting me. That scares me. It should scare you, too.

To reduce these crimes against your children, [former] Texas Governor Ann Richards, for example, advocates more prisons and "harsher" sentences for sex offenders, especially repeat child molesters. Thus she's pushing for more of a solution that does not work, a solution that only means I will take up bed space in one of the many new prisons she is spending millions of dollars on so that later I can commit the same crime. The fact is, prison is nothing more than an oversized, overpriced homeless shelter. Inmates are well fed and clothed and have warm beds to sleep in, all for free. To sex offenders, loss of freedom simply means there are no children available to rape. But we can get child pornography, we can fantasize about the children we watch on television, and we have the memories of our past crimes. Moreover, sex is plentiful in prison. We substitute young-looking partners for children and let our imagination do the rest.

STUDIES FIND CASTRATION IS EFFECTIVE

Why resist the demands of men who are willing to risk sacrificing sexual activity in order to be free of their damaging impulses? Most of the arguments against voluntary castration are based on misconceptions, such as the common belief that it is a barbaric practice that has been used only in Third World countries. The fact is that it has been effectively and humanely used as treatment in Denmark, Czechoslovakia, Holland, Switzerland, Norway, Iceland, Sweden, and Finland. A 1973 Swiss study of a hundred and twenty-one castrated offenders found that the rate of reoffending dropped to 4.1 per cent, compared with 76.9 per cent before the operation. A Danish study in the sixties, which followed as many as nine hundred castrated sex offenders, found that recidivism rates dropped to 2.2 per cent.

New Yorker, March 7, 1994.

Our victims, meanwhile, retain the searing, ghastly memories of abuse, memories that can last a lifetime. Who is punished more?

According to Texas statutes, as well as those of most other states, child molesters currently in prison can be paroled. But a grotesquely high percentage of all untreated sex offenders rape again. Returning us to prison makes us stop—but getting us back in jail means that another child must first fall prey. The system returns a child molester to prison after he is captured by the police, after the child-victim has suffered the torture and savagery of being abused, *after* the child-victim has endured a grueling and humiliating interrogation by strangers. Always after, and always too late to save the child. Our justice system, by releasing criminals like me into communities without effective treatment, now dooms countless children to abuse. And most child rapists get away with raping many children, some over and over before being caught.

A Civilized Alternative

There is a civilized alternative to this tragic cycle: castrate repeat sex offenders.

Now, some good and decent citizens claim that castration itself is barbaric. What is barbaric is what I have done to so many children; refusing to castrate me is barbaric to the children I will molest. *Mandatory* castration of sex offenders, whether for their first, second, or third conviction of a sex offense, is currently a violation of the United States Constitution because it is considered "cruel and unusual punishment." But no punishment is crueler or more unusual than the pain I have caused my victims. *Voluntary* castration is not unconstitutional, but no state allows it.

The governor of Texas, as well as many other state governors, is well aware of the statistics and other information regarding castration, but she turns a deaf ear to my pleas. In doing so, she turns a deaf ear to the children who are my future victims. Criminals who want to be rehabilitated are rare, so it is inconceivable to me that those who volunteer to be castrated are denied this treatment.

I do not write as a scared or worried parent. I have—thankfully—no children at all. I am scared for your children. When they have nightmares, let them be about the ghouls they see in horror movies or on the Saturday morning cartoons. They shouldn't have to have nightmares about me.

My next parole date is June 1995. [McQuay was paroled in April 1996 after serving six years of an eight-year sentence.]

II

Larry Don McQuay was once a child himself. From the innocence of youth, no doubt filled with the promise of life, he became an uncle, step-father, school bus driver, and child molester. A self-proclaimed monster who haunts the nightmares of children, fearful himself of spending eternity in hell, who is Mr. McQuay and what should we do with him?

To be sure, even the mention of castration has an ugly, jarring sound to it; it is an idea that polite people naturally shrink from. But as Mr. McQuay's own words show, there is a terrible problem out there and the ways we are currently trying to solve it aren't working. So if castration, in any form and even in combination with other measures such as counseling, strikes you as the wrong solution, keep thinking about the problem, because everyone can agree that putting people like Mr. McQuay back on the streets is crazy.

HIGH STAKES

Let's be clear about the stakes here. According to the U.S. Department of Health and Human Services, approximately two out of every 1,000 children have been sexually abused, a figure that totaled 138,000 youngsters nationally in 1986. A significant percentage of this figure likely reflects the prevalence of pedophilia in a given community. Because of the driven nature of the disorder, an individual pedophile may make contact with 2 or 3 different children per week, some of the children sometimes being teen-aged prostitutes. This can add up to hundreds of youngsters over a period of several years. Most pedophiles are physically nonviolent.

Let's also be clear about castration. Many people believe that castrating a sex offender is like cutting off the hand of the crook. Not so. Cutting off the penis would be like cutting off the hand of the crook, but that is not what castration is. Surgical castration involves removal of the testes only. When the penis is removed but the testes are still left intact, a man will still try to have sex. If the testes are removed, but the penis left intact, a man is far less likely to attempt to engage in sexual behavior. Removal of the testes generally decreases the desire for sexual activity, rather than affecting the capacity to perform.

The testes are the major source of testosterone production in males. It is the marked elevation in testosterone in males at the time of puberty that is associated with a marked increase in sexual desire and interest. Lowering testosterone can reduce the intensity of sexual desire.

A man can will his right arm to move. He cannot will an erection. He can get an erection by thinking certain thoughts. Tragically, for him and for the rest of us, Mr. McQuay apparently discovered that thoughts and cravings about children are what arouse him. To be afflicted with such a condition can itself be a nightmare. It is a condition that cannot be willed, legislated, or punished away. Reported rates of recidivism in the scientific literature for pedophiles not receiving treatment have varied considerably. It's difficult to know whether a given pedophile has not re-offended or simply re-offended and not been caught. Recidivism rates could, however, be as high as 65 percent. This figure makes intuitive sense: If one goes to prison because of a sexual attraction to 10-year-old boys, there is nothing about being in prison that will erase that attraction.

APPROPRIATE BEHAVIOR

I ask [a convicted rapist, "Steven,"] what it is like to be on Depo-Provera. "Initially, it felt like nothing—it takes about a month for the drug to get into your system. Then I noticed my sexual drive was starting to dissipate a little bit. I wasn't getting erections as often as I was before, and it took longer to get them when I did. I didn't have the urge to masturbate as much as I did before.

"It was strange at first because the will to have sex was still there, but the body wasn't able. They talked to my girlfriend and said I wouldn't want sex the way I had in the past: maybe only once or twice a week. It felt good when I had sex, and I still had the fantasies of coercion. But Depo-Provera allows you the time, mentally, to make the decision about whether this is an appropriate behavior."

Stephen Fried, *Glamour*, June 1995.

The good news is that lowering testosterone levels works. One Danish study reported a 4.3 percent recidivism rate over a period of up to 18 years among 117 surgically castrated sex offenders, whereas 58 noncastrated offenders were 10 times more likely to re-offend. A 7.4 percent recidivism rate was reported among 121 castrated sex offenders in Switzerland over five years compared with a 52 percent rate at the 10 year follow-up among men not undergoing the procedure. Yet another Danish study involving over 900 castrated sex offenders followed for periods of as long as 30 years reported a mere 2.2 percent recidivism rate.

CHEMICAL CASTRATION

Surgical castration, however, is neither necessary nor foolproof. Its effects can be reversed by taking testosterone. A better idea is so-called chemical castration. This involves no surgery—it consists of injections that lower testosterone levels. Compliance with medications used to lower testosterone can readily be monitored because they can be given by means of periodic injections. This treatment recently made headlines. In Florida, a legislative attempt is being made to impose testosterone-lowering injections upon possibly unwilling repeat offenders.

There is precedent in this country for compelling persons to undergo medical procedures without choice. At one time, because of the danger of smallpox, everyone was required to be vaccinated so that they would not pose a danger to the community. Convicted felons lose certain rights (e.g., the right to bear arms). If it were clear that a community would definitely be safer with a sexual offender's testosterone lowered, then society would likely have a right to insist that he make himself safe.

Lowering testosterone is not a cure, a guarantee, or a panacea, but it might be far more palatable to a society in which many people are squeamish about mandating surgical castration. In conjunction with psychological counseling, most testosterone-lowering treatments are effective, especially when used to help individuals who want to change. In combination—chemical castration and counseling—we've seen encouragingly low rates of recidivism; one study found a 15 percent rate, a figure which is deceptively high because the study broadly defined re-offending to include non-sexual contact, like visits to schoolyards.

Today most people still consider sexual offenses, even the many that are nonviolent, to be more a question for the legal system than one in which science and medicine can play a useful role. But like it or not, it is a fact that over 90 percent of incarcerated sex offenders sooner or later will be free. If legislation and punishment alone cannot fully solve the problem, medicine and science need to be called into action. And if society can be made safer by such means, why not use them?

"The motivation for sexual assault will not disappear with the severed genitalia or altered hormones."

CASTRATION OF SEX OFFENDERS WOULD NOT REDUCE SEXUAL VIOLENCE

Daniel C. Tsang and Andrew Vachss

California passed a law in September 1996 requiring certain sex offenders to be castrated after their second offense. In Part I of the following two-part viewpoint, Daniel C. Tsang argues that although chemical castration may lower a sex offender's sex drive, the treatment will not prevent further sex crimes because it does not account for the fact that rape is a crime of violence. In Part II, Andrew Vachss maintains that castration will not remove sex offenders' desire or motivation to rape. Rapists rape because they want to, Vachss contends, not because they are driven by an uncontrollable urge. Castration will not change their motivation, he asserts. Tsang is the author of a chapter on Depo-Provera treatment in the book *Sex, Cells, and Same-Sex Desires*. Vachss is an author, a juvenile justice advocate, and an attorney in New York City.

As you read, consider the following questions:

1. What sex crimes will be exempt from California's castration law, according to Tsang?
2. According to Vachss, why will castration be ineffective against violent sex offenders?
3. How does castration validate a sex offender's feelings about his actions, according to Vachss?

Part I: From Daniel C. Tsang, "A Sex-Crime Law for the Dark Ages," *Los Angeles Times*, September 18, 1996. Part II: From Andrew Vachss, "Sex Offenders: Is Castration an Acceptable Punishment? No: Pragmatically Impotent," *ABA Journal*, July 1992. Reprinted by permission of the *ABA Journal*.

California Gov. Pete Wilson signed into law a bill more appropriate for the Dark Ages than the eve of the 21st century. It mandates surgical castration or drug injections for parolees convicted of sex crimes against children after the second offense (a judge, however, could order chemical castration even with the first offense). This may satisfy the electorate's lust for vengeance, . . . but will do little to stop sexual assaults against children.

A Desperate Cure

Sex offenders could voluntarily choose surgical castration under the new law. Because surgical castration is irreversible, most inmates would probably opt for the lesser of two evils, so-called chemical castration. But Depo-Provera, the hormone-suppressing drug often used to "treat" sex offenders, is a drug that even its proponents never proposed using on violent criminals. In fact, despite assertions of successful treatment in Europe and the anecdotal evidence from true believers, including some ex-cons, the truth is that no one knows what causes men to rape, and forcing Depo-Provera on inmates is akin to the experimentation of Third Reich doctors in Nazi Germany. Depo may or may not lower the "sex drive," but rape is a crime of violence, something that neither chemical nor surgical castration will address.

The enactment of such a law is only the latest in a long and shameful legacy of "great and desperate cures," a term coined by Elliot S. Valenstein, a University of Michigan psychology professor whose 1986 book chronicled experimentation on mental patients and sexual misfits, including psychosurgery on homosexuals, not so long ago.

In England, a BBC-2 television documentary on such "aversion therapy" on homosexuals in the 1960s and 1970s that aired in August 1996 has led the Health Ministry to declare that patients are entitled to compensation from the doctors who treated them. This should remind us that what may be considered legitimate treatment one day may become a significant liability risk the next. In California, in a concession to those troubled by the ethics of such forced treatment, Corrections Department doctors are allowed to opt out of injecting a patient.

The belief that a single drug—in this case, one not cleared by the FDA for such a purpose—can alter abusive behavior is the ultimate in reductionism. Human beings are not automatons propelled solely by "uncontrollable" biological "drives," but are species with highly developed brains. Drugging anyone without his informed consent raises serious constitutional issues; to allow society to do it to prison inmates only raises the question, what or who next?

AN UNCONSTITUTIONAL LAW

The ACLU is likely to challenge the California law as unconstitutional. Case law is on its side. The Michigan Supreme Court already has ruled that requiring Depo-Provera as a condition of probation is "unlawful" because the drug is still experimental for this purpose (it is now primarily used for birth control). The Montana Supreme Court also has barred the use of Depo in forced therapy, a ruling the U.S. Supreme Court did not overturn. And Congress' Office of Technological Assessment, noting that some prison administrators have advocated the use of Depo to control violence and homosexual activity in prisons, has concluded, in a 1988 report, that "such broad and general use of the drug might meet the Supreme Court's test for cruel and unusual punishment: 'shocking to the conscience of reasonably civilized people.'"

Despite the hype, the California law will not do all that the public presumably wants. Not only will it not reduce sex crimes, but it does not cover all sex acts with minors. The law exempts heterosexuals who practice conventional sex on minors. It does not cover males convicted of having vaginal sex with females under 13; it covers only those convicted of sodomy, oral sex, insertion of a foreign object or lewd and lascivious conduct with such minors. Besides, inmates, even after the second offense, will avoid mandatory castration if they are not granted parole.

With this new legislation, California returns to the dark ages of sexual psychopath laws and unfettered collusion between psychiatry and the state. It is ironic that the same Legislature also passed a bill mandating informed consent by women in human egg transfers, in the wake of the UC Irvine fertility scandal. [Fertility doctors are accused of stealing eggs and embryos from some patients to create pregnancies in others.] But those women have a voice; sex offenders are despised and no one will listen to them.

II

As a criminal justice response to the chronic, dangerous sexual psychopath, castration of any kind is morally pernicious and pragmatically impotent. Even if we could ignore the implications of mutilation-as-compensation for criminal offenses, castration must be rejected on the most essential of grounds: The "cure" will exacerbate the "disease."

Proponents of castration tell us: 1) It will heal the offender (and thus protect society), and 2) it would be the offender's own choice.

Voluntary Behavior

Violent sex offenders are not victims of their heightened sex drives. Rapists may be "expressing their rage." Predatory pedophiles may be "replaying their old scripts." But any sexual sadist, properly interviewed, will tell you the truth: They do what they do because they want to do it. Their behavior is not the product of sickness—it is volitional.

Castration will not remove the source of a violent sex offender's rage—only one single instrument of its expression. Rapes have been committed with broomsticks, coke bottles—any blunt object. Indeed, most criminal statutes now incorporate just such a possibility.

An Ineffective Punishment

It might also be effective to cut off the hands of thieves, as the law provides in some Islamic nations. But in American law the effectiveness of a punishment is balanced against the consideration of whether it is inhumane or excessive to the purpose. And in the matter of castration, even its effectiveness is disputed. Though a castrated male will no longer produce semen, he is still capable of an erection. And even men who are incapable of an erection can commit sexual assaults. Most experts regard sexual assault as an act of violence, not desire, an explosion of rage by an attacker who is often dysfunctional at the crucial moment.

Richard Lacayo, Time, March 23, 1992.

And imagine a violent rapist whose hatred of women occupies most of his waking thoughts. Imagine him agreeing to castration to avoid a lengthy prison sentence. Imagine his rage festering geometrically as he stews in the bile of what "they" have done to him. Does anyone actually believe such a creature has been rendered harmless?

An escalating pattern is characteristic of many predatory sex offenders—castration is likely to produce an internal demand for even higher levels of stimulation.

The castration remedy implies some biomedical cause for sexual offenses. Once fixed, the offender ceases to be a danger. This is nonsense—the motivation for sexual assault will not disappear with the severed genitalia or altered hormones.

In Germany, Klaus Grabowski avoided a life sentence by agreeing to castration. Released, he began covert hormone injections. In 1980, he strangled a 7-year-old girl and buried her body. At trial, his defense was that the castration had removed any sexual feelings, that he had lured the child to his apartment because he loved children and killed her in response to blackmail threats.

High Predatory Drive

Even the most liberal of Americans have become suspicious of a medical model to explain sex offenders. Such offenders may plot and plan, scheme and stalk for months, utilize the most elaborate devices to avoid detection, even network with others and commercially profit from their foul acts.

But some psycho-apologist can always be found to claim the poor soul was deep in the grip of irresistible impulse when he was compelled to attack. Imagine the field day the expert-witness fraternity will have explaining how the castrated child molester who later killed his new victims was rendered insane as a result of the castration itself.

Sex offender treatment is the growth industry of the 1990s. Chemical castration already looms as a Get-Out-of-Jail-Free Card.

Castration validates the sex offender's self-portrait: He is the victim; he can't help himself. It panders to our ugliest instincts, not the least of which is cowardice—the refusal to call evil by its name.

Choice Is Not a Defense

Nor can castration be defended because the perpetrator chooses it. Leaving aside the obvious issue of coercion, under what theory does a convicted criminal get to select his own (non-incarcerative) sentence?

America loves simple solutions to complex problems, especially solutions with political utility, like boot camp for youthful offenders. The last thing our cities need is muggers in better physical shape.

When it comes to our own self-interest (and self-defense), the greatest sickness is stupidity. Castration qualifies . . . on all counts.

| "Citizens who know their neighbors will be safer than those who don't."

COMMUNITY NOTIFICATION LAWS WILL REDUCE SEXUAL VIOLENCE

Tucker Carlson

Community notification laws require that residents be informed when a convicted sex offender moves into a neighborhood. In the following viewpoint, Tucker Carlson contends that criminals are more likely to commit crimes in areas where they are not known. When neighbors are aware that a convicted sex offender lives among them, he argues, they can keep their children out of harm's way. Furthermore, Carlson asserts, community notification laws ensure that the offender will know he or she is being watched and will therefore refrain from participating in illegal behavior. Carlson is a Bradley Fellow at the Heritage Foundation, a conservative public policy institute.

As you read, consider the following questions:

1. Who may be hurt by community notification laws, in Carlson's opinion?
2. What is the recidivism rate for parolees and probationers, according to the author?
3. How many Americans were on parole or probation in 1993, according to Carlson?

Excerpted from Tucker Carlson, "Thy Neighbor's Rap Sheet," Policy Review, Spring 1995. Copyright 1995 by The Heritage Foundation. Reprinted by permission of The Heritage Foundation.

On New Year's Eve 1975, after an evening of taking LSD and watching cop shows on television, 15-year-old Raul Meza showed up at a convenience store near his house in Austin, Texas, armed with a deer rifle. Meza emptied the cash register, then marched the clerk, a 20-year-old college student named Derly Ramirez, into the walk-in freezer. Meza shot him in the back and left him for dead.

Ramirez recovered to testify against the man who wounded him. Meza received a 20-year sentence, and served five years before getting out on parole.

STRIKE TWO

On January 3, 1982, months after his release, 21-year-old Raul Meza abducted Kendra Page, a third-grader, as she rode her bicycle near her home in southeast Austin. Meza tortured, raped, and strangled the girl, then left her body behind a dumpster. Three days later, he surrendered to the police. Meza received 30 years for the killing.

While behind bars, Meza racked up demerits for various infractions, and four years were added to his sentence after guards found a knife in his cell. Meza came up for parole seven times, and each time it was denied.

By 1993, however, prison authorities could keep Meza no longer. Under Texas law, he had accumulated enough credit for good behavior to qualify automatically for release. The state freed him under mandatory supervision, a conditional release not unlike parole that can be granted without the consent of the parole board.

No matter how notorious, most felons leave prison with little fanfare. They re-enter society quietly and soon become anonymous. Some begin new and honest lives. Many others, freed from supervision and accountable to no one, commit new crimes. Raul Meza might have regained his freedom in the same way. But he never got the chance. One hundred and forty miles from Meza's Huntsville prison cell, an Austin newspaper editor decided to make him famous.

In 15 years of covering crimes, Jerry White, the city editor of the *Austin American-Statesman*, had watched scores of criminals disappear from public view after sentencing. Most of them left prison years before their sentences expired, often to rob, rape, or kill again. "It became apparent," says White, "that even though these folks are sentenced and sent away, the story doesn't really end." White began compiling a list of inmates who were "fairly notorious" in Austin. Every few months, he called the department of corrections to ask when inmates on his list would be eligible for parole.

In June 1993, the department of corrections confirmed that Meza was due to be released soon. Using the state's Open Records Act, the newspaper petitioned Texas's attorney general and found where Meza planned to live. An article ran on the front page of the Sunday paper eight days before Meza's release. The headline read, "'Nothing's Going to Stop It': Killer of 8-Year-Old About to Be Freed."

CONSTANT MEDIA ATTENTION

In a city of about 465,000 people, the story reached 240,000 homes and provoked an outpouring of media attention. Film crews greeted Meza as he walked out of the state prison and followed him for months. Publicity, mostly bad, seemed to trail him everywhere. Corrections officials moved him from town to town, but in each residents and local politicians protested his presence. Colin Amann, a Houston lawyer who represented the killer after his release, says angry citizens "kicked him in the butt from one end of Texas to the other."

For much of 1993, Texans kept on kicking. Over several months, he was shuttled between towns and cities all over the state. Of the 276 halfway houses that were asked to accept Meza, 271 refused. "Every town he went to," says Amann, "people were just screaming and yelling. Lots of small communities went out and bitched about it. A lot. And it happened every time they'd move him, they had the same outcry."

In August 1993, the parole division placed Meza on his grandparents' farm, west of San Antonio. On August 31, local sheriffs charged Meza with "terroristic threatening" and disorderly conduct for bullying his elderly grandparents. A judge later dismissed the charges, but the incident made nearly every newspaper in Texas. At least 1,000 local residents signed a petition asking the state to move Meza again. The parole division sent him to Austin.

STRIKE THREE

His new neighbors protested, held rallies, carried signs. A few moved away. The furor subsided a bit when the father of the murdered girl publicly called for citizens to give Meza the chance to start a new life. He moved into his mother's house and found a job. In the first 10 months of 1994, the *American-Statesman* ran more than 20 stories on Meza. In August 1994, he was arrested for violating the curfew provision of his parole, and he returned to the state prison in Huntsville.

At the time Meza was taken into custody, there were more than 116,000 parolees in Texas, 15,000 of whom had outstanding warrants for parole violations. Yet the governor's fugitive squad focused its energies on Meza, the most famous one. And while parolees in Texas routinely get three chances to break parole before being arrested, Meza was taken into custody after only one violation. His supporters cried foul. But the citizens of Texas were the better for it.

Thompson/Copley News Service. Reprinted with permission.

Meza needed all the attention he could get. As a group, violent sex offenders have an extraordinarily high rate of recidivism. In Texas, about one-third of convicted rapists are arrested for new crimes within two years of getting out on parole. Ordinarily, parole officers are not able to supervise sex offenders carefully. But because they learned from news reports where Meza lived, neighbors were able to keep their children out of his path. Relentless publicity forced a troubled parole system to work effectively. And information disseminated by the press helped to create thousands of civilian parole officers—watchful neighbors who kept an eye on him.

Publicity, however, is a blunt instrument, and others were unintentionally bludgeoned by Meza's fame. His relatives were humiliated. His victim's parents saw their tragedy replayed in the press. And Meza himself was hounded across the state. Nobody knows how such attention may have retarded his rehabilitation, but it may not matter. Despite the burdens imposed on him and his family—or, more likely, because of them—Meza did not kill another child while out of prison.

Even Meza's attorney, a self-described liberal, believes the publicity was worth the cost. "I think everybody should know when a parolee is coming to live in their neighborhood," says Colin Amann. "That's why crime is committed, because people don't know who the criminals are. Once they get out, let's let the entire world know where they are going to live. Let's let the community have some responsibility for keeping its thumb on them."

KNOWLEDGE AND SAFETY

More and more communities are clamoring for that very responsibility. Meza's case illustrates what most people already sense: Citizens who know their neighbors will be safer than those who don't. Study after study has shown anonymity to be a factor in many crimes. Simply put, criminals are more apt to commit crimes in neighborhoods where they do not know the neighbors, and where the neighbors do not know one another. As James Q. Wilson and Richard Herrnstein explain in *Crime and Human Nature*, their expansive survey of criminology, "the more rapid the population turnover in an area, the higher the victimization rate, even after controlling for the racial and age composition."

Conversely, close-knit communities tend to be resistant to predatory crime. A criminal is less likely to commit crimes where the neighbors recognize him, particularly if they know that he has a criminal record.

Statistics explain why citizens have a vested interest in knowing who in their neighborhood has been convicted of serious offenses. Ex-cons commit a staggering amount of crime. As John DiIulio of Princeton University has pointed out, "within three years of sentencing, while still on probation, nearly half of all probationers are placed behind bars for a new crime or abscond." Nationally, recidivism for parolees is about the same as for probationers. DiIulio cites a revealing study of Florida convicts.

"Between 1987 and 1991, about 87 percent of the 147,000 felons released from Florida prisons were released early. Fully one-third of these parolees committed a new crime. At points in time when they would have been incarcerated had they not been released early, these parolees committed nearly 26,000 new crimes, including some 4,656 new crimes of violence—346 murders, 185 sexual assaults, 2,369 robberies, and 1,754 other violent offenses."

Megan's Law

From now on, every State in the country will be required by law to tell a community when a dangerous sexual predator enters its midst. We respect people's rights, but today America proclaims there is no greater right than a parent's right to raise a child in safety and love. Today, America warns: If you dare to prey on our children, the law will follow you wherever you go, State to State, town to town.

Today, America circles the wagon around our children. Megan's Law will protect tens of millions of families from the dread of what they do not know. It will give more peace of mind to our parents.

Bill Clinton, May 17, 1996.

Not only are felons on supervised release dangerous, but there are a lot of them. In 1993, according to the Bureau of Justice Statistics, a total of 671,000 Americans were on parole or probation. There is considerable evidence that many parole and probation officers are responsible for far more offenders than they can possibly supervise, even those housed under one roof. An investigation in 1993 by the *Rocky Mountain News* found that one of every six convicted felons placed in Colorado halfway houses escaped. That year, the study found, 526 felons walked away from halfway houses and into the surrounding neighborhoods. Seven of the escapees were convicted murderers. "In most cases," the paper concluded, "no one looked for them."

Neighbors Can Help

Informed neighbors don't always just keep offenders from committing crimes; sometimes they can help ex-cons straighten out. Mike Elsworth got out of prison in Washington, D.C., for the last time on Halloween 1990, after serving two years for selling cocaine. Elsworth, who was paroled to the same part of town where he grew up, credits his neighbors for helping him keep his record clean since his release. Although he was shunned by at least one woman on his block, other "neighbors were supportive and understanding of me trying to do better once I got out. They knew I was looking for a job, and they would tell me about places that they knew were hiring, and some of them would tell me if I needed anything to come on by." Three months after his release, with the encouragement of his neighbors, Elsworth found a job.

Elsworth says his neighbors gave him the help and attention his parole officers did not. In two years, Elsworth reported to five different officers. "It was like, every three months I had a new one," he says, "I don't know why. They really had little or no concern about me as a person." Elsworth met with his parole officer for 10 to 15 minutes every few weeks. But he saw his neighbors every day, which ultimately, he says, made all the difference.

4

| "[Community notification laws] won't rehabilitate child molesters, which is the action society needs to take to guard youngsters."

COMMUNITY NOTIFICATION LAWS WILL NOT REDUCE SEXUAL VIOLENCE

James Breig

Community notification laws—which require residents to be notified if a convicted child molester moves into their neighborhood—will not protect children from child molesters, contends James Breig in the following viewpoint. In order to protect children from child molesters, he argues, parents must teach children about the world's dangers and society must provide treatment for sex offenders. Furthermore, Breig maintains, community notification laws are unconstitutional because they extend a convict's punishment beyond the court-imposed sentence. Breig is a freelance writer and editor of the *Evangelist*, a diocesan newspaper of Albany, New York.

As you read, consider the following questions:

1. What is Megan's Law, according to the author?
2. For what three reasons is Megan's Law a bad law, according to the author?
3. In Breig's opinion, how should society treat sex offenders?

From James Breig, "Labeling Sex Offenders Won't Protect Your Kids," *U.S. Catholic*, November 1996. Reprinted with permission from *U.S. Catholic*, published by Claretian Publications, 205 W. Monroe St., Chicago, IL 60606.

Jesse K. Timmendequas is not the sort of person you want to know, much less have as a neighbor. Now 35, he has spent at least the past 15 years either sexually abusing children or serving time for doing so. He has confessed twice to child molestation, and one judge called him a "compulsive, repetitive sexual offender."

In 1994, according to the police and prosecutors in New Jersey, Timmendequas preyed on another little girl, 7-year-old Megan Kanka. This time, they say, his brutality did not stop at sexual abuse; this time, he murdered his victim. Megan, it turned out, had Timmendequas as a neighbor. When he and two other sex offenders were released from prison, they moved into her community of Hamilton, New Jersey. The authorities did not inform the Kankas or anyone else on the block that the ex-convicts were coming. One day, police report, Timmendequas lured Megan away by promising her the chance to pet a puppy. Once he had her alone, he strangled her.

AN UNJUSTIFIABLE LAW

The justifiable outrage that followed Megan's death has led to an unjustifiable law named for her, first on a state level and then in federal legislation, signed in May 1996 by President Clinton. "Megan's Laws," as the statutes have come to be known, require authorities to notify communities when a child molester is released into their midst. An example is New York State's Megan's Law, officially known as the Sex Offender Registration Act. Under its provisions, offenders must register with the state's Division of Criminal Justice Services within ten days of being released from prison. Some offenders must then verify their home address annually for ten years. High-risk offenders must keep in touch every 90 days. When Governor George Pataki signed the law early in 1996, he declared: "This will make New York's communities safer for our children."

He's wrong. So is the law. The best intentions—and they abound in the case of victimized children and their pained survivors—don't always result in good laws. Megan's Law is an example. It won't resurrect Megan or protect her peers. It certainly won't rehabilitate child molesters, which is the action society needs to take to guard youngsters. Warning parents about a potential threat to their children is a worthwhile goal, but Megan's Law is so unconstitutional that it can't survive a serious challenge in the courts. A federal judge has already blocked enforcement of the New Jersey version of the law on which the laws of other states have been modeled. Once Megan's Law has been removed from the books, as it inevitably will be, society will be back where it started. Maybe then it will direct its rage in the proper direction: toward taking some serious action to deal with sex offenders rather than opting for quick fixes and bad laws.

WHY THE LAW IS WRONG

It's not difficult to see why the federal judge has put the brakes on Megan's Law. First of all, it unjustly continues the punishment of the person after he or she has served time. Released from prison, a person is labeled by the state of New York as either a level-one, -two, or -three risk, which determines who will be told about his or her crimes. Level-three persons have to register for life; they will not only have information about their crimes disseminated but also have their exact addresses given to the public, in much the same way that red meat is given to leopards. Some people want punishment to continue beyond the prison walls because, they rightly complain, offenders are released too early from prison. Sentenced to ten years for one of his offenses, for example, Timmendequas was paroled after serving only a few months. Such foreshortened punishment is ineffective and should be ended, but it does not justify extending penalties past the walls of prison.

COMMUNITY NOTIFICATION

Source: Reprinted by permission of Kirk Anderson.

A second reason such laws are wrong is that they pick out one specific group of criminals for special treatment. Why select only child molesters for such public labeling? Why not burglars? I'd sure like to know when one of them moves in next door. Wouldn't you want to know if your new neighbor is given to selling drugs or stealing cars or destroying property? If so, then be prepared to explain why we shouldn't pin a list of sins and crimes on you, too. Such scarlet letters would allow everyone to know what you've done—and might do again. The people you deal with on a daily basis at work might appreciate knowing that you are quick to anger or slow to forgive or have a roving eye or a foul mouth.

A FALSE SENSE OF SECURITY

But what is most wrong about Megan's Law does not involve constitutionality; it involves morality. First, the law provides a false sense of security. Every community already has child molesters in them. It is a parent's duty—albeit a sad one—to teach his or her children properly about strangers, the dangers of the world, and how to protect themselves. If parents begin to believe that the state is doing that education for them, they will drop their guard and abandon one of their most important duties toward their children: teaching them about the reality of sin and evil in the world. None of us likes to tell our children that there are bad people in the neighborhood, but we must; it is part of their moral upbringing.

There is another moral problem at the heart of Megan's Law: it is an attempt to avoid admitting the truth about our ignorance about the causes and cures of sexual abuse. We don't know what to do with child molesters because we don't understand what makes them the way they are. We don't know why Timmendequas and his ilk prey on children; we can't comprehend it, and they can't explain themselves. The compulsion they are under is overwhelming; and even when they look for help, there is little to be found. We easily label them, to use the words of several New York politicians, as "fiends, monsters, and predators," but we shy away from taking the more difficult road of offering counseling and making sure they take part in it as a condition of their release from prison.

Faced with such lack of understanding and inability to treat the problem, we resort to the legal equivalent of leeches. Until psychology advances enough to help us treat sex offenders, we are embarrassed by their existence among us. So we try to shun them. The same sort of labeling was tried a few years ago with drunk drivers, who were ordered to drive cars with license plates that identified them. It didn't lower deaths from drunk driving. What does work are immediate punishment, effective treatment programs, and aftercare.

A QUICK FIX

With child molesters, we've got the punishment part down (if we make sure to keep them in prison longer); it's the treatment and aftercare that we've fumbled. In desperation, we reach for quick fixes like Megan's Law. While that will help us point a finger at someone, it will also distract us from protecting our children from those offenders we don't know and prevent us from providing the help that could turn a twisted individual into someone with the self-respect that leads to respect for others.

The horrible death of Megan Kanka, the terrible suffering of her family, the lingering fear in their community—all of that should be harnessed to produce something more effective, constitutional, and moral than Megan's Law. She deserves better. And as Christians called to witness repentance, forgiveness, and reconciliation by a Lord who showed us how when he healed lepers, forgave a condemned criminal, and told an adulteress to sin no more, we have to add that Jesse K. Timmendequas deserves better, too.

It's easy, Jesus said, to love the Megans of the world. He will judge us on how we loved the Jesses.

"There are probably only a few thousand highly dangerous sex criminals in the country. These laws are a way to keep them out of circulation."

SEXUAL PREDATOR LAWS CAN REDUCE SEXUAL VIOLENCE

John Leo

Indeterminate sentencing allows the criminal justice system to keep a sex offender who is judged to be a danger to the community imprisoned indefinitely, even after the original sentence is served. In the following viewpoint, nationally syndicated columnist John Leo contends that many sex offenders are sexual predators—career rapists and child molesters who repeatedly commit new crimes when they are released from prison. Leo argues that indeterminate sentencing is the only way society can protect itself from those who are determined to rape and molest repeatedly.

As you read, consider the following questions:

1. How many offenses do rapists and child molesters commit before they are arrested, according to Leo?
2. How does indeterminate sentencing protect a prisoner's rights, in Leo's opinion?
3. How many men were being held under indeterminate sentencing laws in 1994, as cited by the author?

From John Leo, "Dealing with Career Predators," *U.S. News & World Report*, April 11, 1994. Copyright 1994, U.S. News & World Report. Reprinted with permission.

The tiny Northern California town of Alturas is in an uproar over the presence of a parolee named Melvin Carter in a nearby work camp. Carter, a former engineer from Colorado, confessed to raping about a hundred women in his first dozen years as a California resident. Convicted of 12 of those rapes, he was sentenced to 25 years in prison and actually served 12½ years.

Much of the outrage about Carter is of the NIMBY [Not In My Back Yard] variety. "We refuse to be the dumping ground for another county's hazardous waste," said one resident. Carter was dumped in a rural area because he liked to target single women in college towns, and Gov. Pete Wilson, up for reelection, wanted him "out in the wilderness someplace." But behind the NIMBY issue is a more important social question: Why would any sane society release a hundred-victim career rapist anywhere at any time?

A Revolving Door

By now we are numb to the folly of a system that keeps putting dangerous sexual offenders back on the streets. Warren Bland had a 26-year career of sexual attacks and torture, but the state of California let him go five times, finally convicting him and putting him on death row for mutilating and killing a 7-year-old girl. Richard Allen Davis, "a monstrous personality," according to one criminologist, was let go again and again before he kidnapped and killed Polly Klaas. In both these cases, and in many others, authorities were warned early that they were dealing with very dangerous predators. A psychiatrist said that Bland would be "assaultive and/or homicidal toward women" if released, and a probation officer pointed early to Davis's "accelerating potential for violence."

The revolving door works so fast that when a new wave of rapes occurs, police know to hunt suspects among the freshly paroled. Testifying before Congress in March 1994, Linda Fairstein, head of the sex crimes prosecution unit in Manhattan, N.Y., spoke about a recent series of rapes of young girls and said she and her staff "would be very surprised" if the perpetrator didn't turn out to be a known sex offender. That very day, New York police arrested and charged a convicted rapist in the crimes. The man had been released from prison six months before the rape spree began.

Price to Pay

The social cost of letting career predators go every few years is enormous. According to a recent study, rapists and child molesters are arrested once for every 30 offenses they commit. So even if every arrest results in conviction, an average of 30 new victims will be created before each serial sex criminal goes back to jail for a while.

The public's revulsion over this sort of folly has been a long time coming, but now it's here. More and more, states are requiring released sex criminals to register with authorities when they move into a new area. The *New Yorker* magazine has come out for voluntary castration of sex offenders as an alternative to jail time. The Senate of the state of Florida in the Spring of 1994 recommended "chemical castration"—regular drugs to suppress testosterone—for twice-convicted rapists. (This won't happen, but it's an accurate indicator of the public's outrage.)

VICTIMS' RIGHTS

Washington's "Sexual Predator" law, . . . enacted in the wake of a sensational 1989 child mutilation case, permits the state to lock up indefinitely any convicted violent sex offender—after he has served his time. Since it was passed, Washington has confined 15 "predators." None has been charged with or even suspected of committing a new crime. Instead, the state contends the men's criminal histories demonstrate that they have a "mental abnormality" requiring confinement until they can be successfully treated. . . .

Backers of the predator law say it is a statute for the 1990s, reversing previous trends and putting victims' rights ahead of the rights of criminals. Correctly administered, they say, the law is a legal "rifle shot" aimed at getting proven sex offenders off the street. Nonpredators are protected by a winnowing-out process that includes the state board, a prosecutor and a jury, supporters say. "If you use it right," says Vernon Quincey, a professor of psychology at Canada's Queens University who has reviewed the program, "it is possible to have a pretty good hit rate."

Bill Richards, *Wall Street Journal*, December 8, 1992.

There's a better way to go: sexual predator laws, combined with a return to indeterminate sentencing. Berkeley, Calif., criminologist Jerome Skolnick argues that Davis, freed after the mandated six years for his first set of offenses, would likely have been kept much longer under an indeterminate sentence. It's not always easy to spot the serious long-term offender early. But once the pattern is seen, a long sentence is crucial.

Davis would almost certainly have been held under a predator law like the one in Washington State, which allows authorities to detain and evaluate a predator after his term is complete. A court at that point determines whether he is to be kept off the streets as a danger to the community.

PREVENTIVE DETENTION

It's a form of preventive detention, which ought to make us all at least a bit uncomfortable. And because the law has a light dusting of pseudo-psychiatric language, critics have compared it to the Soviet Union's use of psychiatry to control dissidents. But a community has the right to defend itself from predators, and the law provides a trial at which a prisoner's rights are balanced by the community's right to public safety.

Under a predator law, testimony on the continuing danger of people like Bland and Davis could be introduced as evidence. And so could comments by predators that they intend to strike again after release. In cases of gruesome sexual assault in New Jersey and Minnesota, for instance, officials scrambled for ways to keep offenders off the streets after hearing of their plans to attack again.

Despite fears that authorities would overpredict dangerousness, as of April 1994 only 16 men are being held under the law, seven are awaiting trial and one was released. The legislation has been upheld by the state Supreme Court. No doubt it will one day wend its way to the U.S. Supreme Court. But for now, it seems to be working as intended. Predator laws are probably the wave of the future. There are probably only a few thousand highly dangerous sex criminals in the country. These laws are a way to keep them out of circulation.

| "If you can stash [a sex offender] in jail forever . . . , you can do the same to any other offender, regardless of how heinous or harmless he is."

SEXUAL PREDATOR LAWS ARE UNCONSTITUTIONAL

Samuel Francis

Career rapists and molesters who exhibit no willingness to change their behavior are deemed sexual predators and a danger to the community by several states. These states allow sexual predators to receive indeterminate sentences—indefinite prison terms that keep them imprisoned until they are judged to no longer be a danger to the community, even if it means detaining them after their original sentence has been served. In the following viewpoint, Samuel Francis argues that sexual predator laws are unconstitutional. He maintains that by imposing exceptional penalties on sexual predators, such laws violate the requirement that all people be treated equally under the law. Francis contends that if sexual predators can be imprisoned indefinitely, then the rights of everyone else are also jeopardized. Francis is a nationally syndicated columnist.

As you read, consider the following questions:
1. What is the "whole point" of law, according to the author?
2. What case inspired Washington's sexual predator law, according to Francis?
3. In the author's opinion, why are sexual predators not executed?

S ex crime makes great politics, and the state of Washington has come up with a dumb little law that helps politicians far more than it hurts rapists and child molesters. Late in 1992, the *Wall Street Journal* carried an article about the law and how other states are getting ready to copy it.

INDEFINITE PRISON SENTENCES

Under a statute that supporters claim is a "rifle shot" aimed at deviants who repeatedly attack women and children, convicted offenders can be kept in prison indefinitely—long after they've served their full sentences. The *Journal* cites the case of one Vance Cunningham, whose life consists of sexual attacks on one woman after another since he was 15. Now he's confined to the state slammer, maybe forever.

He's already served the sentence for rape he was given in 1989, but under Washington's "sexual predator" law, a panel of 10 decided he needed to remain locked up. When and if he will get out neither he nor the panel nor anyone else knows. He and other convicts classified as "mentally abnormal" will stay as guests of the state until they are "successfully treated."

The law excites misinformed citizens who imagine that it really makes it tough on criminals, and it also causes politicians to salivate. Five other states think the law is terrific, and they're waiting for the courts to decide on its constitutionality before drafting similar statutes.

What few seem to grasp is that the statute is a direct attack on the concept of the rule of law as well as on the even more fundamental concept of moral responsibility and punishment. Today it locks up sex offenders; tomorrow, recidivist red-light runners.

Under quaint notions like the rule of law, citizens know what they can and cannot legally do as well as what will and will not happen to them if they break laws. The whole point of law is to provide permanent standards by which citizens, as well as the state, can regularize their conduct according to known rules.

Moreover, citizens are assumed to possess sufficient moral responsibility to merit punishment if they violate known rules, and even to deserve rewards if they do something heroic or especially virtuous. Under the headshrinker justice Washington offers, both concepts have been pitched out. If you can stash characters like Cunningham in jail forever on the supposition that he's too abnormal to behave himself outside of jail, you can do the same to any other offender, regardless of how heinous or harmless he is.

Nor does the practice ensure toughness on crime. Cunningham may stay in jail forever, and given the seriousness of his offenses, no one will much miss him. But by the same logic that keeps him in jail until doomsday, a panel of shrinks and social workers could decide that killers like Charles Manson are rehabilitated after a few months on the jailhouse witch doctor's couch. Citizens who fantasize that the sexual predator statute will keep killers and rapists behind bars are fooling themselves.

SOMETHING MUST BE DONE

The Washington law originated in 1989, after the notorious case of Earl Shriner crawled into the light. Shriner is a lifelong sex offender who assaulted a 7-year-old boy and cut off his penis. In prison, he boasted of his plans to attack others after he was released.

The Shriner case led the people of Washington to descend on their Legislature and demand that something be done. The legislators went into a huddle and came up with the sexual predator law. That may not have been what the citizens had in mind. The mother of the boy whom Shriner assaulted says, "A lot of people said, 'Why do we need these guys anyway? Why not just kill them?'" Well, why not indeed?

HUMAN BEHAVIOR IS NOT PREDICTABLE

One of criminal law's toughest dilemmas [is] how to balance society's need for protection from rapacious monsters against an individual's constitutional rights. We put people in prison for what they've done, not for what they might do based on a menacing remark or diabolic biography—at least that's long been the tradition in Anglo-American law. Suspicion is fine to get a search warrant or tail a Camaro, but not enough for jail time. "Nobody, except God, is able to predict human behavior," says Prof. Norval Morris of the University of Chicago law school.

David A. Kaplan, *Newsweek*, January 18, 1993.

The reason why not is that politicians just can't bring themselves these days to visit simple justice on human cobras like Shriner and Cunningham. They have to replace justice with therapy. But everyone except the legislators, apparently, knows how to deal with them.

The Washington law, its supporters claim and the *Journal* reports, is "a statute for the 1990s, reversing previous trends and putting victims' rights ahead of the rights of criminals." This, of course, is nonsense.

Voodoo Justice

The sexual predator law is the fulfillment of a century-long trend of replacing justice and law with psychiatry and therapy. It not only guts the rights of those who suffer under it now but also jeopardizes the rights of everyone else. It's the final stage of a morally collapsed society whose leaders are afraid to punish because they've forgotten the simple difference between right and wrong.

Washington can keep its voodoo justice if it wants, but the people of other states ought to start telling their elected leaders how to tell the difference and what that difference teaches about how creatures like Cunningham and Shriner ought to be treated.

> "As long as traditional sex-role stereotypes and attitudes remain, so probably will rape."

GENDER EQUALITY WOULD REDUCE RAPE

Julie A. Allison and Lawrence S. Wrightsman

In the following viewpoint, Julie A. Allison and Lawrence S. Wrightsman argue that traditional attitudes and values regarding the role and status of women contribute to a social environment that encourages rape. When men are more powerful than women, the authors contend, women face a higher risk of rape. In order to prevent rape, the authors maintain, women must be given access to more power and the public must be educated about sex-role stereotypes. Allison and Wrightsman are the authors of *Rape: The Misunderstood Crime*, from which this viewpoint is excerpted.

As you read, consider the following questions:

1. What are three approaches to preventing rape, according to the authors?
2. What evidence do Allison and Wrightsman present to support their contention that progress is being made in changing attitudes about rape?
3. What are the two types of societal response to rape, according to Mary P. Koss and Mary R. Harvey, as cited by the authors?

A woman from Edinburgh, Scotland, tells an interviewer:

Over the years, my awareness of the possibility of rape has dawned on me so much that I'm a lot more fearful of going out at night on my own. Sometimes, I won't even go out in the day if I know its [sic] an isolated place. It seems crazy that it's only dawned on me now and not in my teens or early twenties. I haven't been raped, but now I live in fear, and it drains me to even think about it. The realization that it can happen almost anywhere is crucifying. In the past, I've hitched alone, lived alone in quiet places, and gone to isolated places alone. Now I do none of these things. I feel my sense of freedom to be crushed, while men do not experience this fear. Their allowance of freedom sickens me.

How does one avoid being raped? Is the above strategy the only solution? Certainly these are important questions for both the public and researchers to ask. Unlike the questions, which seem so straightforward and simple, there is no one simple answer. Many aspects are involved and must be considered, and even after such review, any answer must come in qualified form. For example, when someone asks, "How can I avoid being raped?" is she asking how to avoid being attacked, or how to avoid being raped, once an attack begins?

PREVENTING RAPE

"Preventing" rape is a broad umbrella, and—as Mary P. Koss and Mary R. Harvey observe—the aims of specific rape prevention strategies can include any number of diverse goals, including the following:

1. to eliminate the act of rape by scrutinizing those beliefs, values, and myths of our society that perpetuate and condone sexual assault;
2. to deter attempted rapes by educating potential victims about avoiding risks and defending themselves; . . .

Research motivated to answer potential victims' questions has been multifaceted in an effort to reflect the importance of many determinants in preventing rape. This viewpoint will be organized around three approaches: the individual's response in preventing rape, the role of the situation, and society's place in the instigation and discouragement of rape. Although each of these is discussed separately, in real life these aspects cannot be disentangled.

The individualistic approach to avoiding rape examines aspects of the potential rape victim, including what she or he may do in order to secure personal safety. Research that has used this level of analysis has, as an example, looked at personal factors of rape victims and the behaviors that potential rape victims could employ to avoid rape. This approach, on occasion, places the responsibility for avoiding victimization solely on the potential victim, and therefore runs the risk of creating an environment conducive to blaming the victim. For some, the following is a logical development: if there are actions one can take to avoid being raped, then if one is raped, one is responsible. It is therefore extremely important to remember that often one only knows in hindsight whether a particular response was successful. And a successful response used by one individual may prove to be futile for another. . . .

PUBLIC POLICY INITIATIVES

The likelihood of violence may . . . be influenced by legislative initiatives that seek to redress gender-based power imbalances, including legislation on women's reproductive rights, pay equity, dependent care and family support, and civil rights legislation. Active efforts to help women move into jobs traditionally held by men, to eliminate discrimination in hiring and training, to move women into leadership positions, and to create a prowomen climate through policies such as family leave and child care assistance, can all be considered part of a comprehensive attack on the conditions that underlie and foster male violence against women.

Mary P. Koss et al., *No Safe Haven*, 1994.

In contrast, the situational approach to avoiding rape focuses on identifying situations that may place individuals at a higher risk of being raped. For example, is rape more likely to be avoided when an attack takes place in the open, as opposed to an attack within the confines of four walls? Does alcohol play a role in the risk of rape? Certain situations place an individual at a higher risk of being raped. Like the individual approach, however, the fact that there are identifiable situations that may be more "rape-prone" does not mean that if an individual is raped in this particular situation, the victim somehow deserved to be raped because of being in the situation.

Finally, the third conceptual approach to avoiding rape treats rape as a societal problem that can be effectively treated only by community awareness and involvement. This approach considers rape as a human issue, rather than just a women's issue or a men's issue. The Central Park "wilding" incident in Manhattan [in which a gang of youths raped and beat a woman jogger in 1989] and the gang rape [in the poolroom of a bar in 1984] in New Bedford, Massachusetts, make us aware that rape is a community concern. The goals of this approach include educating society in an attempt to nullify the existence of rape myths, as well as altering the imbalanced power structure between men and women. To use Koss and Harvey's analogy, this approach emulates a public health model in that it seeks "to eliminate the environmental conditions that promote disease and to inoculate all or all at-risk members of the population against disease." . . .

THE SOCIETAL APPROACH

The United States might be considered a rape-prone society. Traditional attitudes and values, as well as the alarming amount of violence in general, and sexual violence specifically, all point to this conclusion. To be considered a potentially rape-prone society, however, does not mean that this must be a permanent status. To address the problem of rape on a societal level, one must examine the power differential between women and men, the attitudes traditionally held in society that perpetuate the myths about rape, and the education programs that have recently begun.

Until recently, little attention has been given to the societal approach, partly because it is difficult to demonstrate the effects of such factors on behavior. But in the last few years, more systematic analyses have emerged. For example, Barry R. Burkhart and Mary Ellen Fromuth have identified three specific societal mechanisms that affect rape incidence and hence inhibit its prevention:

1. gender role socialization patterns and power differentials that normalize rape by advancing rape-supportive beliefs
2. sexually coercive cognitive schemata and beliefs that encourage the tendency to blame the victim, and reduce society's capacity to empathize, and
3. social-sexual interaction scripts that prescribe norms about courtship.

According to James A. Doyle, no evidence has been produced that a truly egalitarian society exists—one in which men and women are considered equal. And there is not, nor has there ever been, a matriarchal society, where women controlled the resources of society. Hence, the only possibility for true equality between the sexes—and the removal of the differential power structure—rests in its potential in the future. Because research suggests that ascribing more power to males in society increases the risk of rape for women, removing such barriers to power for women should decrease such a risk. It is up to society—and those who hold positions of power—to take responsibility for removing such barriers.

PROGRESS

Some progress has been made on this area. Fraternities, for example, are beginning to respond to the problem of gang rape, which has been found to occur all too often on college campuses—especially in fraternities.

The Supreme Court, in *New York State Club Association, Inc. v. City of New York* (1988), ruled unanimously that a city may bar sex and race discrimination in large clubs where members make important business and professional contacts. And some large corporations, such as IBM, are increasing their employee benefit options that allow up to 3 years of unpaid leave for such purposes as caring for a new baby, sick child, or elderly relative, without the threat of losing one's employment status.

SOCIETAL AND INSTITUTIONAL AWARENESS

Women should let men know when their behavior is offensive. But individual complaints are toothless without societal and institutional awareness, dialogue, and censure. The feminist movement that Camille Paglia and others vilify has brought about these critical societal attitudes and structures. For just one example, look to the way rape victims are now treated by the police. When rape victims go to the police they can now hope to be met with respect, thanks to feminist efforts to sensitize officers, many of whom didn't take the crime seriously before.

Helen Cordes, *Utne Reader*, January/February 1993.

Some have suggested that the power differential between women and men in nearly all societies, which has been documented for centuries, created sex-role stereotypes as a justification for treating women differently. As long as traditional sex-role stereotypes and attitudes remain, so probably will rape. Attitudes may play [a large role] in both the likelihood to rape and the condoning of aggression between the sexes. Social change takes time, and such beliefs or behaviors are not expected to change overnight. Indeed—such efforts to change began with the women's movement in the early 1970s. We believe that stronger acceptance of truly egalitarian values is not an impossible goal and would lead to less sexual violence committed against women.

Jacquelyn W. White and Susan B. Sorenson describe how pervasive sex-role stereotypes have even influenced the study of rape itself. Until the advent of the women's movement, research on rape was primarily done by male investigators from a clinical perspective rather than one reflecting an awareness of societal forces. The emphasis was on the diagnosis of rapists; as White and Sorenson note, the experiences of victims were almost irrelevant in the early stage. More recently, the emphasis has shifted to the experiences of women and victims.

Societal Contributions to Rape Prevention

But as we have noted earlier, this more recent focus runs the risk of perpetuating concepts of victim blame. White and Sorenson urge that research focus on the context of sexual assault; that is, greater analysis of societal contributions to the prevention of rape.

All of these changes must be made through education and awareness in order ultimately to prevent rape. Daniel Linz, Barbara S. Wilson, and Edward Donnerstein, for example, call for educational interventions specifically designed to change beliefs about rape and sexual violence. Some of this is going on—in the media, in popular magazines, and through the efforts of crisis centers and schools.

Koss and Harvey distinguish between two types of societal response. Approaches that employ *environmental action* include community education programs, "Take Back the Night" marches, and school-based or university-based awareness programs. Approaches focusing on *citizen inoculation* seek to develop both self-defense competencies in those at risk and values and beliefs incompatible with rape in others. It is too early to establish the effectiveness of such initiatives but at the very least they should reduce the status of rape as a misunderstood crime.

No Easy Solution

There is no easy solution to preventing rape. The experts are unclear about the "best" strategy to use to prevent rape because there is no best strategy. However, research that has studied victims who have been attacked have found that those who used more active strategies were generally more likely to avoid being raped. Still, this does not solve the problem of preventing the possibility of attack. To do that requires focusing our attention not on potential victims, but on the situations that create vulnerabilities for rape, on potential rapists, and on society in general.

Ultimately, if we as a society are going to prevent rape, we have to understand it. Even though it is possible to come to an understanding of rape, we do not see that rape is justifiable.

Rape is a crime, it is an act of violence, and its consequences are dramatic. To attempt to prevent rape by focusing on the behavior of the victim serves to perpetuate the myths and misconceptions about rape. Ultimately, we need to hold all individuals responsible for their own behavior. It must be recognized that rape is a behavior for which rapists must be held accountable. Society as a whole must recognize that all violence, including rape, is unacceptable behavior.

"It's a woman's personal responsibility now ... to make herself physically fit, so that she can fight off as best she can man's advances."

WOMEN ARE RESPONSIBLE FOR REDUCING RAPE

Camille Paglia, interviewed by Celia Farber

Camille Paglia is the author of the controversial books *Sexual Personae* and *Sex, Art, and American Culture*. In the following viewpoint, which is excerpted from a two-part interview by Celia Farber for *Spin* magazine, Paglia maintains that women must accept their responsibility for rape. According to Paglia, rape is a risk that comes with the freedom to experience life at its fullest. A woman must avoid dangerous situations if she does not want to be raped, Paglia argues.

As you read, consider the following questions:

1. According to Paglia, why are women the dominant sex?
2. How does rape compare to murder, in Paglia's opinion?
3. What is the main quality women have that they are not using, in Paglia's view?

From Camille Paglia, two-part interview by Celia Farber, SPIN, September and October 1991. Reprinted by permission of Camoflage Associates, New York.

Paglia: I'm noticing that many people coming into the media now are people whose minds have been poisoned by their training at Yale and other Ivy League places. For example, I see where this whole date-rape thing is coming from. I recognize the language of these smart girls who are entering the media; they are coming from these schools. They have this stupid, pathetic, completely-removed-from-reality view of things that they've gotten from these academics who are totally off the wall, totally removed. Whereas my views on sex are coming from the fact that I am a football fan and I am a rock fan. Rock and football are revealing something true and permanent and eternal about male energy and sexuality. They are revealing the fact that women, in fact, like the idea of flaunting, strutting, wild masculine energy. The people who criticize me, these establishment feminists, these white upper-middle-class feminists in New York, especially, who think of themselves as so literate, the kind of music they like, is, like Suzanne Vega—you know, women's music.

Spin: Yuck.

DATE-RAPE PROPAGANDA

Paglia: This date-rape propaganda has been primarily coming out of the elite schools, where the guys are all these cooperative, literate, introspective, sit-on-their-ass guys, whereas you're not getting it that much down in the football schools where people accept the fact of the beauty and strength of masculinity. You see jocks on the campus all the time—they understand what manhood is down there. It's only up here where there is this idea that they can get men on a leash. It's these guys in the Ivy League schools who get used to obeying women. They're sedentary guys. It's ironic that you're getting the biggest bitching about men from the schools where the men are just eunuchs and bookworms.

Spin: That point about primordial male sexuality is also at odds with much contemporary pop psychology. I'm referring to the twelve-step, women-who-love-too-much school of thought, which insists that a woman's attraction to an "untamed" man, as it were, is necessarily a sign of sickness—a sign of a warped emotional life that invariably traces back to childhood, and the attention span of the father. It never considers such an attraction to be a naturally occurring phenomenon—a force of nature. I think the approach to remedying the problem is simplistic, even dangerously so at times.

Paglia: I agree. I'm a Freudian. I like Freud very much, even though I adapt him and add things to him. But his system of analysis is extremely accurate. It's a conflict-based system that allows for paradox. It's also very self-critical and self-analytical. I've watched therapy getting more and more mushy in the past fifteen years in America. . . . It's become what I call coercive compassion. It's disgusting, it's condescending, it's insulting, it's coddling, it keeps everyone in an infantile condition rather than in the adult condition that was postulated as the ultimate goal of Freudian analysis. You were meant to be totally self-aware as a Freudian. Now, it's everyone who will help you, the group will help you. It's awful. It's a return to the Fifties conformist model of things. It's this victim-centered view of the world, which is very pernicious. We cannot have a world where everyone is a victim. "I'm this way because my father made me this way. I'm this way because my husband made me this way." Yes, we are indeed formed by traumas that happened to us. But then you must take charge, you must take over, you are responsible. Personal responsibility is at the heart of my system. But today's system is this whining thing, "Why won't you help me, Mommy and Daddy?" It's like this whole thing with date rape.

THE DOMINANT SEX

Spin: One point that hasn't been made in the whole rape debate is women's role over men, sexually. In the case of a rape, a man has to use brute force to obtain something that a woman has— her very sex. So naturally she's weaker physically, and will always be oppressed by him physically. But in that moment when he decides that the only way he can get what he wants from her emotionally, or sexually, or whatever, is to rape her, he is confessing to a weakness that is all-encompassing. She is abused, but he is utterly tragic and pathetic. One is temporary and the other is permanent. I was raped once and it helped me to think of it like that. Not at all to apologize for him, but to focus on my power instead of my helplessness. It was a horrible experience, but it certainly didn't destroy my whole life or my psyche, as much as contemporary wisdom insisted it must have.

Paglia: Right, we *have* what they want. I think woman is the dominant sex. Men have to do all sorts of stuff to prove that they are worthy of a woman's attention. It's very interesting what you said about the rape, because one of the German magazine reporters who came to talk to me—she's been living in New York for ten years—she came to talk to me about two weeks ago and she told me a very interesting story, very similar

We must reconsider how we raise our children. I believe that the pattern of sexual harassment that begins in grade school could be altered if we taught our daughters to fight back when attacked by boys. We expect girls to be comforted with the admonition not to pay them any mind; boys are like that. In other words: get used to it.

If more boys received more negative reinforcement at the hands of girls, the offensive behavior might be discouraged. At the very least, girls would feel less powerless. If there really is a war against women, then we ought to be raising women warriors.

Adele M. Stan, *New York Times*, December 17, 1993.

---

to yours. She lives in Brooklyn, and she let this guy in whom she shouldn't have, and she got raped. She said that, because she's a feminist, of course she had to go for counseling. She said it was awful, that the minute she arrived there, the rape counselors were saying, "You will never recover from this, what's happened to you is so terrible." She said, what the hell, it was a terrible experience, but she was going to pick herself up, and it wasn't that big a deal. The whole system now is designed to make you feel that you are maimed and mutilated forever if something like that happens. She said it made her feel worse. It's absolutely American—it is not European—and the whole system is filled with these clichés about sex. I think there is a fundamental prudery about sex in all this. Rape is one of the risk factors in getting involved with men. It's a risk factor. It's like driving a car. My attitude is, it's like gambling. If you go to Atlantic City—these girls are going to Atlantic City, and when they lose, it's like "Oh, Mommy and Daddy, I lost." My answer is stay home and do your nails, if that's the kind of person you are. My Sixties attitude is, yes, go for it, take the risk, take the challenge—if you get raped, if you get beat up in a dark alley in a street, it's okay. That was part of the risk of freedom, that's part of what we've demanded as women. Go with it. Pick yourself up, dust yourself off, and go on. We cannot regulate male sexuality. The uncontrollable aspect of male sexuality is part of what makes sex interesting. And yes, it can lead to rape in some situations. What feminists are asking for is for men to be castrated, to make eunuchs out of them. The powerful, uncontrollable force of male sexuality has been censored out of white middle-class homes. But it's still there in black culture, and in Spanish culture.

PART TWO

Spin: In the first part of our interview, the section about rape upset every single woman who read it—in the offices at *Spin* and even at the typesetters. They all seemed to feel that you were defending the rapist.

Paglia: No, that's not it at all. The point is, these white, upper-middle-class feminists believe that a pain-free world is achievable. I'm saying that a pain-free world will be achievable only under totalitarianism. There is no such thing as risk-free anything. In fact, all valuable human things come to us from risk and loss. Therefore we value beauty and youth because they are transient. Part of the sizzle of sex is the danger, the risk of loss of identity in love. That's part of the drama of love. My generation demanded no more overprotection of women. We wanted women to be able to freely choose sex, to freely have all the adventures that men could have. So women began to hike on mountain paths and do all sorts of dangerous things. That's the risk of freedom. If women break their legs on mountain bikes, that's the risk factor. I'm not defending the rapist—I'm defending the freedom to risk rape. I don't want sexual experience to be protected by society. A part of it is that since women are physically weaker than men, in our sexual freedom, women are going to get raped. We should be angry about it, but it's a woman's personal responsibility now, in this age of sexual liberation, to make herself physically fit, so that she can fight off as best she can man's advances. She needs to be alert in her own mind to any potential danger. It's up to the woman to give clear signals of what her wishes are. If she does not want to be out of control of the situation, she should not get drunk, she should not be in a private space with a man whom she does not know. Rape does not destroy you forever. It's like getting beaten up. Men get beat up all the time.

Spin: But don't you think that people see a man getting beat up and a woman getting raped as completely different? Do you think rape should be considered as serious a crime as murder?

THE PROPER ATTITUDE ABOUT SEX

Paglia: That's absurd. I dislike anything that treats women as if they are special, frail little creatures. We don't need special protection. Rape is an assault. If it is a totally devastating psychological experience for a woman, then she doesn't have a proper attitude toward sex. It's this whole stupid feminist thing about how we are basically nurturing, benevolent people, and sex is a wonderful thing between two equals. With that kind of attitude, then of course rape is going to be a total violation of your entire life, because you have had a stupid, naïve, Mary Poppins view of life to begin with. Sex is a turbulent power that we are not in control of; it's a dark force. The sexes are at war with each other. That's part of the excitement and interest of sex. It's the dark realm of the night. When you enter the realm of the night, horrible things can happen there. You can be attacked on a dark street. Does that mean we should never go into dark streets? Part of my excitement as a college student in the Sixties was coming out of the very protective Fifties. I was wandering those dark streets understanding that not only could I be raped, I could be killed. It's like the gay men going down to the docks and having sex in alleyways and trucks; it's the danger. Feminists have no idea that some women like to flirt with danger because there is a sizzle in it. You know what gets me sick and tired? The battered-woman motif. It's so misinterpreted, the way we have to constantly look at it in terms of male oppression and tyranny, and female victimization. When, in fact, everyone knows throughout the world that many of these working-class relationships where women get beat up have hot sex. They ask why she won't leave him? Maybe she won't leave him because the sex is very hot. I say we should start looking at the battered-wife motif in terms of sex. If gay men go down to bars and like to get tied up, beaten up, and have their asses whipped, how come we can't allow that a lot of wives like the kind of sex they are getting in these battered-wife relationships? We can't consider that women might have kinky tastes, can we? No, because women are naturally benevolent and nurturing, aren't they? Everything is so damn Mary Poppins and sanitized.

WOMEN'S SEXUAL POWERS

Spin: What do you think is the main quality that women have within them that they aren't using?

Paglia: What women have to realize is their dominance as a sex. That women's sexual powers are enormous. All cultures have seen it. Men know it. Women know it. The only people who don't know it are feminists. Desensualized, desexualized, neurotic women. I wouldn't have said this twenty years ago because I was militant feminist myself. But as the years have gone on, I begin to see more and more that the perverse, neurotic psychodrama projected by these women is coming from their own problems with sex.

Periodical Bibliography

The following articles have been selected to supplement the diverse views presented in this chapter. Addresses are provided for periodicals not indexed in the *Readers' Guide to Periodical Literature*, the *Alternative Press Index*, the *Social Sciences Index*, or the *Index to Legal Periodicals and Books*.

Anonymous	"Confessions of a Child Molester," *On the Issues*, Winter 1995.
Brian Bergman	"Pedophile Alert," *Maclean's*, March 20, 1995.
Andrea Bernstein	"Should You Be Told That Your Neighbor Is a Sex Offender?" *Ms.*, November/December 1995.
Peter Davis	"The Sex Offender Next Door," *New York Times Magazine*, July 28, 1996.
Midge Decter	"Megan's Law & the 'New York Times,'" *Commentary*, October 1994.
Sarah Glazer	"Punishing Sex Offenders," *CQ Researcher*, January 12, 1996. Available from 1414 22nd St. NW, Washington, DC 20037.
Erica Goode	"Battling Deviant Behavior," *U.S. News & World Report*, September 19, 1994.
André Henderson	"The Scariest Criminal," *Governing*, August 1995.
Paul Kaihla	"Sex Offenders: Is There a Cure?" *Maclean's*, February 13, 1995.
Wendy McElroy	"The New Mythology of Rape," *Liberty*, September 1994. Available from PO Box 1181, Port Townsend, WA 98368.
Stephanie N. Mehta	"Treating Sex Offenders Becomes an Industry, but Does It Work?" *Wall Street Journal*, May 24, 1996.
New York Times	"Dealing with Sex Offenders," August 15, 1994.
Psychology Today	"Rape: To Fight or Not to Fight," May/June 1994.
Anastasia Volkonsky	"Legalizing the 'Profession' Would Sanction the Abuse," *Insight*, February 27, 1995. Available from 3600 New York Ave. NE, Washington, DC 20002.

FOR FURTHER DISCUSSION

CHAPTER 1

1. R. Barri Flowers and Robert T.M. Phillips argue that pornography and rap music, respectively, objectify and demean women and influence some men to act in a sexually aggressive manner toward women. Marcia Pally contends that men rape not because they have been exposed to rap music and pornography, but because they want to hurt their victims. Based on the viewpoints, which argument do you think is strongest? Why?

2. Harry Allen maintains that advertising alcoholic beverages—which are proven to be associated with a variety of social ills—is much more harmful to the black community than is rap music. Although rap is alleged to demean women and provoke violence, Allen asserts it is merely a way for blacks to talk about what is happening to and around them. Do you agree with his argument? Why or why not? Robert T.M. Phillips contends that rap music desensitizes its listeners to violence, making them more likely to act violently toward women and others in the future. Do you agree? Why or why not?

3. This chapter lists several possible causes of sexual violence. Consider each alternative and then list arguments for and against the validity of each one. Note whether the arguments are based on facts, values, emotions, or other considerations. If you do not believe an alternative is a valid cause of sexual violence, explain why.

CHAPTER 2

1. Neil Gilbert maintains that many researchers have exaggerated the prevalence of rape on college campuses. Paula Kamen takes issue with Gilbert's contention. Does Kamen's viewpoint effectively refute Gilbert's argument? Why or why not?

2. Laura M. Markowitz argues that victims of childhood incest often block out conscious memories of sexual abuse, while Claudette Wassil-Grimm contends that many "recovered" memories of childhood sexual abuse are false. What evidence does each author present to support her argument? Which author's use of evidence do you find more convincing? Why?

CHAPTER 3

1. Mary Gaitskill believes that it is important for victims of sexual violence to face their feelings about being victimized. She discusses her own rape experiences to help support her con-

clusions. How does her use of personal testimony influence your opinion of her viewpoint? Are you persuaded by her argument? Why or why not?

2. Carol Tavris asserts that therapists and self-help books for incest survivors have caused many adults to wrongly conclude that they were sexually abused as children. Ellen Bass and Laura Davis refute Tavris's contention, arguing that the problem of sexual violence against children is more prevalent than most Americans generally assume. Which viewpoint do you most strongly agree with, and why?

3. Abbe Smith argues that expert testimony on battered woman syndrome should be allowed at jury trials involving women accused of killing their abusive husbands. Michael Weiss and Cathy Young contend that the existence of self-defense laws negates the need for such testimony in most cases. Compare the opinions presented in these two viewpoints, then formulate your own argument about the feasibility of testimony on battered woman syndrome.

CHAPTER 4

1. Larry Don McQuay, a convicted child molester, argues that the only way to keep him from molesting more children when he is released from prison is to castrate him. Daniel C. Tsang, a social scientist, and Andrew Vachss, a juvenile justice advocate, maintain that castration cannot change human behavior or motivation and therefore is not a legitimate treatment. What evidence do each of their viewpoints offer to support these arguments? Which argument seems stronger? Why? Do the backgrounds of the authors influence your assessment of their arguments? Explain.

2. Camille Paglia asserts that if a woman does not want to be raped, she must avoid situations where rape is a possibility, such as being alone with a man she does not know or becoming drunk. Do you agree with her argument? Why or why not?

ORGANIZATIONS TO CONTACT

The editors have compiled the following list of organizations concerned with the issues debated in this book. All of them have publications or information available for interested readers. For best results, allow as much time as possible for the organizations to respond. The descriptions below are derived from materials provided by the organizations. This list was compiled upon the date of publication. Names, addresses, phone and fax numbers, and e-mail and Internet addresses of organizations are subject to change.

Center for the Prevention of Sexual and Domestic Violence (CPSDV)
936 N. 34th St., Suite 200, Seattle, WA 98103
(206) 634-1903 • fax: (206) 634-0115
e-mail: cpsdv@cpsdv.seanet.com • Internet: http://www.cpsdv.org

CPSDV is an educational resource center that works with both religious and secular communities throughout the United States and Canada to address the issues of sexual abuse and domestic violence. The center offers workshops concerning sexual misconduct by clergy, spouse abuse, child sexual abuse, rape, and pornography. Materials available from the CPSDV include the quarterly newsletter *Working Together* and the books *Sexual Abuse Prevention: A Course of Study for Teenagers*, *Violence Against Women and Children*, and *Sexual Violence: The Unmentionable Sin*.

Center for Women Policy Studies (CWPS)
1211 Connecticut Ave. NW, Suite 312, Washington, DC 20036
(202) 872-1770 • fax: (202) 296-8962

CWPS is an independent feminist policy research and advocacy institution established in 1972. The center studies policies affecting the social, legal, health, and economic status of women. Available publications include fact sheets on violence against women and girls and the report *Violence Against Women as Bias-Motivated Hate Crime: Defining the Issues*.

Emerge: Counseling and Education to Stop Male Violence
2380 Massachusetts Ave., Suite 101, Cambridge, MA 02140
(617) 422-1550 • fax: (617) 547-0904

Emerge is a victim-advocacy organization that works to prevent domestic violence, including sexual violence, by providing training workshops to counselors and counseling services to batterers. It also conducts research and disseminates information. Publications available from Emerge include the articles "Counseling Men Who Batter: A Pro-feminist Analysis of Treatment Models" and "The Addicted or Alcoholic Batterer."

False Memory Syndrome Foundation (FMSF)
3401 Market St., Suite 130, Philadelphia, PA 19104-3315
(215) 387-1865 • (800) 568-8882 • fax: (215) 387-1917

Members of the foundation believe that many "delayed memories" of sexual abuse are the result of false memory syndrome (FMS), which they say is caused by therapists' mistakenly implanting false memories of traumatic experiences in the minds of their patients. The foundation seeks to discover reasons for the spread of FMS, works for the prevention of new cases, and aids FMS victims, including those falsely accused of sexual abuse. The foundation publishes the FMS Foundation Newsletter and various working papers and distributes articles and information on FMS.

Family Research Laboratory (FRL)
University of New Hampshire
126 Horton Social Science Center, Durham, NH 03824-3586
(603) 862-1888 • fax: (603) 862-1122
Internet: http://www.unh.edu/frl/index.html

FRL is an independent research unit devoted to the study of the causes and consequences of family violence. It also works to dispel myths about family violence through public education. It publishes numerous books and articles on violence between men and women, spouse/cohabitant abuse, marital rape, and verbal aggression. The organization's World Wide Web site offers a complete listing of available materials, including the article "Child Sexual Abuse and Pornography: Is There a Relationship?" and the book Four Theories of Rape in American Society: A State-Level Analysis.

Incest Resources (IR)
Cambridge Women's Center
46 Pleasant St., Cambridge, MA 02139
(617) 354-8807

IR provides educational and resource materials for incest survivors. The center is an information referral service that also offers support groups for people victimized by sexual harassment and incest. The IR legal packet is a series of articles and resource listings related to civil prosecution of incest offenders. A self-addressed, stamped envelope (two first-class stamps) must accompany requests for information.

Incest Survivors Resource Network International (ISRNI)
PO Box 7375, Las Cruces, NM 88006-7375
(505) 521-4260
e-mail: ISRNI@zianet.com • Internet: http://www.zianet.com/ISRNI

ISRNI is a Quaker-operated networking and educational resource center dedicated to the prevention of incest. ISRNI offers numerous publications, sponsors conferences, and operates a helpline staffed solely by incest survivors.

National Center for Missing & Exploited Children (NCMEC)
2101 Wilson Blvd., Suite 550, Arlington, VA 22201-3052
(703) 235-3900 • toll-free hotline: 1-800-THE-LOST
fax: (703) 235-4067
e-mail: ncmec@cis.compuserve.com
Internet: http://www.missingkids.org

NCMEC is a private organization funded by the Department of Justice. The center serves as a clearinghouse of information on missing and exploited children and coordinates child protection efforts with the private sector. The center also maintains a 24-hour hotline that callers can use to report child pornography and sightings of missing children. Available publications include guidelines for parents whose children are testifying in court, child safety information, and books such as *Children Traumatized in Sex Rings* and *Child Molestors: A Behavioral Analysis*.

National Coalition Against Censorship (NCAC)
275 Seventh Ave., New York, NY 10001
(212) 807-6222 • fax: (212) 807-6245
e-mail: NCAC@netcom.com

NCAC is an alliance of organizations committed to defending freedom of thought, inquiry, and expression by engaging in public education and advocacy on the national and local levels. The coalition promotes the belief that the censorship of violent and sexual materials represses intellectual and artistic freedom. NCAC maintains a library of information dealing with First Amendment issues. It publishes the quarterly *Censorship News* and various reports, including "The Sex Panic: Women, Censorship, and 'Pornography.'"

National Coalition for the Protection of Children & Families
800 Compton Rd., Suite 9224, Cincinnati, OH 45231
(513) 521-6227 • fax: (513) 521-6337
e-mail: ncpcf@nationalcoalition.org
Internet: http://www.nationalcoalition.org

Formerly known as the National Coalition Against Pornography, the coalition is an alliance of civic, business, religious, health care, and educational groups working to stop the violence that they believe is promoted by obscenity and child pornography. It assists citizens in enforcing laws against child pornography and obscenity; it also helps draft legislation to initiate or strengthen existing anti-obscenity laws. The coalition's publications include *Children, Pornography, and Cyberspace* and *Pornography: A Human Tragedy*.

National Coalition of Free Men
PO Box 129, Manhasset, NY 11030
(516) 482-6378
e-mail: ncfm@liii.com • Internet: http://www.ncfm.org

The coalition's members include men seeking "a fair and balanced perspective on gender issues." The organization promotes men's legal rights in issues such as false accusation of rape, sexual harassment, and sexual abuse. It conducts research, sponsors educational programs, maintains a database on men's issues, and publishes the bimonthly *Transitions*.

National Institute of Justice (NIJ)
U.S. Department of Justice
National Criminal Justice Reference Service
PO Box 6000, Rockville, MD 20849-6000
(800) 851-3240
e-mail: askncjrs@ncjrs.org

The NIJ, the research and development agency of the U.S. Department of Justice, was established to prevent and reduce crime and to improve the criminal justice system. It provides studies and statistics on child rape victims, child victimizers, and violence against women. Among its publications are the reports "The Criminal Justice and Community Response to Rape" and "When the Victim Is a Child."

NOW Legal Defense and Education Fund
99 Hudson St., New York, NY 10013
(212) 925-6635 • fax: (212) 226-1066
Internet: http://www.nowldef.org

The NOW Legal Defense and Education Fund is a branch of the National Organization for Women (NOW). It is dedicated to the eradication of sex discrimination through litigation and public education. The organization offers a list of publications on rape, incest, and sexual abuse, as well as a legal resource kit on child sexual abuse.

Office for Victims of Crime Resource Center
Box 6000, Rockville, MD 20850
(800) 627-6872

Established in 1983 by the U.S. Department of Justice's Office for Victims of Crime, the resource center is a primary source of information regarding victim-related issues. It answers questions by using national and regional statistics, research findings, and a network of victim advocates and organizations. The center distributes all Office of Justice Programs (OJP) publications, including *Female Victims of Violent Crime* and *Sexual Assault: An Overview*.

People Against Rape (PAR)
PO Box 5876, Naperville, IL 60567
(800) 877-7252
e-mail: Personal_Empowerment_Programs@msn.com

People Against Rape primarily seeks to help teens and children avoid becoming the victims of sexual assault and rape by providing instruction in the basic principles of self-defense. PAR further promotes self-esteem and motivation of teens and college students through educational programs. Publications include *Defend: Preventing Date Rape and Other Sexual Assaults* and *Sexual Assault: How to Defend Yourself*.

Sex Information and Education Council of the U.S. (SIECUS)
130 W. 42nd St., Suite 350, New York, NY 10036-7802
(212) 819-9770 • fax: (212) 819-9776
e-mail: SIECUS@siecus.org • Internet: http://www.siecus.org

SIECUS is a clearinghouse for information on sexuality, with a special interest in sex education. It publishes sex education curricula, the bimonthly newsletter *SIECUS Report*, and fact sheets on sex education issues. Its articles, bibliographies, and book reviews often address the role of sex education in identifying, reducing, and preventing sexual violence.

Survivor Connections (SC)
52 Lyndon Rd., Cranston, RI 02905-1121

Survivor Connections is an activist organization for survivors of sexual assault. It provides referrals to attorneys, therapists, and peer support groups. The organization also seeks to educate the public about legislation affecting survivors and encourages criminal prosecution and civil claims against perpetrators. A quarterly newsletter, the *Survivor Activist*, is available to the general public.

Survivors of Incest Anonymous (SIA)
PO Box 21817, Baltimore, MD 21222-6817

(410) 282-3400

Established in 1982, Survivors of Incest Anonymous is a twelve-step self-help recovery program for victims of incest. The organization provides national and international support groups, bulletins, and speakers; it also publishes the pamphlets *Incest: The Family Tragedy* and *Must We Forgive?*

VOCAL/National Association of State VOCAL Organizations (NASVO)
7485 E. Kenyon Ave., Denver, CO 80237

(303) 233-5321 • (303) 770-5096 • (800) 745-8778

VOCAL (Victims of Child Abuse Laws) provides information, research data, referrals, and emotional support to those falsely accused of child abuse, including sexual abuse. NASVO maintains a library of research on child abuse, focusing on legal, psychological, social, and medical issues, and will provide photocopies of articles for a fee. It publishes the monthly *NASVO/VOCAL Colorado Newsletter*.

VOICES in Action (Victims of Incest Can Emerge Survivors)
PO Box 148309, Chicago, IL 60657

(773) 327-1500 • (800) 786-4238

e-mail: voices@voices-action.org

VOICES in Action assists victims of childhood sexual abuse through support, networking, education, and promoting public awareness. The organization offers workshops, audio tapes of conference presentations, and the bimonthly newsletter the *Chorus*.

BIBLIOGRAPHY OF BOOKS

Beverly Allen — *Rape Warfare: The Hidden Genocide in Bosnia-Herzegovina and Croatia*. Minneapolis: University of Minnesota Press, 1996.

Julie A. Allison and Lawrence S. Wrightsman — *Rape: The Misunderstood Crime*. Newbury Park, CA: Sage Publications, 1993.

Louise Armstrong — *Rocking the Cradle of Sexual Politics: What Happened When Women Said Incest*. Reading, MA: Addison-Wesley, 1994.

Howard E. Barbaree, William L. Marshall, and Stephen M. Hudson, eds. — *The Juvenile Sex Offender*. New York: Guilford Publications, 1993.

Ola W. Barnett and Alyce D. LaViolette — *It Could Happen to Anyone: Why Battered Women Stay*. Thousand Oaks, CA: Sage Publications, 1993.

Ellen Bass and Laura Davis — *The Courage to Heal: A Guide for Women Survivors of Child Sexual Abuse*. New York: HarperPerennial, 1994.

Sandra Lipsitz Bem — *The Lenses of Gender: Transforming the Debate on Sexual Inequality*. New Haven, CT: Yale University Press, 1993.

Helen Benedict — *Virgin or Vamp: How the Press Covers Sex Crimes*. New York: Oxford University Press, 1992.

Raquel Kennedy Bergen — *Wife Rape: Understanding the Response of Survivors and Service Providers*. Thousand Oaks, CA: Sage Publications, 1996.

Carol Bohmer and Andrea Parrot — *Sexual Assault on Campus: The Problem and the Solution*. New York: Lexington Books, 1993.

Emilie Buchwald, Pamela Fletcher, and Martha Roth, eds. — *Transforming a Rape Culture*. Minneapolis: Milkweed Editions, 1993.

Efua Dorkenoo — *Cutting the Rose: Female Genital Mutilation: The Practice and Its Prevention*. London: Minority Rights Publications, 1994.

Donald G. Dutton — *The Batterer: A Psychological Profile*. New York: Basic-Books, 1995.

Warren Farrell — *The Myth of Male Power: Why Men Are the Disposable Sex*. New York: Simon & Schuster, 1993.

R. Barri Flowers	*The Victimization and Exploitation of Women and Children*. Jefferson, NC: Mcfarland, 1994.
Rus Ervin Funk	*Stopping Rape: A Challenge for Men*. Philadelphia: New Society Publishers, 1995.
Eleanor Goldstein and Kevin Farmer	*Confabulations: Creating False Memories, Destroying Families*. Boca Raton, FL: SIRS Books, 1992.
Gordon C. Nagayama Hall	*Theory-Based Assessment, Treatment, and Prevention of Sexual Aggression*. New York: Oxford University Press, 1996.
Robert D. Hare	*Without Conscience: The Disturbing World of the Psychopaths Among Us*. New York: Pocket Books, 1993.
Philip Jenkins	*Pedophiles and Priests: Anatomy of a Contemporary Crisis*. New York: Oxford University Press, 1996.
Wendy Kaminer	*I'm Dysfunctional, You're Dysfunctional: The Recovery Movement and Other Self-Help Fashions*. Reading, MA: Addison-Wesley, 1992.
Mary P. Koss et al.	*No Safe Haven: Male Violence Against Women at Home, at Work, and in the Community*. Washington, DC: American Psychological Association, 1994.
Wayne Kritsberg	*The Invisible Wound: A New Approach to Healing Childhood Sexual Abuse*. New York: Bantam Books, 1993.
Edward O. Laumann et al.	*The Social Organization of Sexuality: Sexual Practices in the United States*. Chicago: University of Chicago Press, 1994.
Sharice A. Lee	*The Survivor's Guide: For Teenage Girls Surviving Sexual Abuse*. Thousand Oaks, CA: Sage Publications, 1995.
Elizabeth Loftus and Katherine Ketcham	*The Myth of Repressed Memory*. New York: St. Martin's Press, 1994.
Nan Bauer Maglin and Donna Perry, eds.	*"Bad Girls"/"Good Girls": Women, Sex, and Power in the Nineties*. New Brunswick, NJ: Rutgers University Press, 1996.
Cynthia L. Mather and Kristina E. Debye	*How Long Does It Hurt? A Guide to Recovery from Incest and Sexual Abuse for Teenagers, Their Friends, and Their Families*. San Francisco: Jossey-Bass, 1994.

James Randall Noblitt and Pamela Sue Perskin	*Cult and Ritual Abuse: Its History, Anthropology, and Recent Discovery in Contemporary America.* Westport, CT: Praeger, 1995.
Richard Ofshe and Ethan Watters	*Making Monsters: False Memories, Psychotherapy, and Sexual Hysteria.* New York: Scribner, 1994.
Mark Pendergrast	*Victims of Memory: Incest Accusations and Shattered Lives.* Hinesburg, VT: Upper Access Books, 1995.
Douglas W. Pryor	*Unspeakable Acts: Why Men Sexually Abuse Children.* New York: New York University Press, 1996.
Katie Roiphe	*The Morning After: Sex, Fear, and Feminism on Campus.* New York: Little, Brown, 1993.
Diana E.H. Russell	*Against Pornography: The Evidence of Harm.* Berkeley, CA: Russell Publications, 1993.
Beth Sipe and Evelyn J. Hall	*I Am Not Your Victim: Anatomy of Domestic Violence.* Thousand Oaks, CA: Sage Publications, 1996.
Adele M. Stan	*Debating Sexual Correctness: Pornography, Sexual Harassment, Date Rape, and the Politics of Sexual Equality.* New York: Dell, 1995.
Alexander Stiglmayer	*Mass Rape: The War Against Women in Bosnia-Herzegovina.* Lincoln: University of Nebraska Press, 1994.
Nadine Strossen	*Defending Pornography: Free Speech, Sex, and the Fight for Women's Rights.* New York: Scribner, 1995.
Carolyn F. Swift, ed.	*Sexual Assault and Abuse: Sociocultural Context of Prevention.* New York: Haworth Press, 1995.
James T. Tedeschi and Richard B. Felson	*Violence, Aggression, and Coercive Actions.* Washington, DC: American Psychological Association, 1994.
Lenore Terr	*Unchained Memories: True Stories of Traumatic Memories, Lost and Found.* New York: BasicBooks, 1994.
Alice Vachss	*Sex Crimes.* New York: Random House, 1993.
Alice Walker and Pratibha Parmar	*Warrior Marks: Female Genital Mutilation and the Sexual Blinding of Women.* New York: Harcourt Brace, 1993.
Colleen A. Ward	*Attitudes Toward Rape.* Thousand Oaks, CA: Sage Publications, 1995.
Robin Warshaw	*I Never Called It Rape: The Ms. Report on Recognizing, Fighting, and Surviving Date and Acquaintance Rape.* New York: HarperPerennial, 1994.

Claudette
Wassil-Grimm

Diagnosis for Disaster: The Devastating Truth About False Memory Syndrome and Its Impact on Accusers and Families. Woodstock, NY: Overlook Press, 1995.

Vernon R. Wiehe and
Ann L. Richards

Intimate Betrayal: Understanding and Responding to the Trauma of Acquaintance Rape. Thousand Oaks, CA: Sage Publications, 1995.

Naomi Wolf

Fire with Fire: The New Female Power and How It Will Change the Twenty-first Century. New York: Random House, 1993.

INDEX